Concentration and Meditation

Mother —
This is about the best
introduction to the general
subject — the general practice —
I've ever come across. Particularly
parts 1 & 2. You might also read
chapter 12 on Zen.
I don't know much about
yoga, but if you want to read
more about Zen, tell me, because
I have many things.

Love —
David.

CHRISTMAS HUMPHREYS

CONCENTRATION

AND

MEDITATION

A MANUAL OF
MIND DEVELOPMENT

THE CLEAR LIGHT SERIES

1969
SHAMBALA
BERKELEY

PUBLISHED BY SHAMBALA PUBLICATIONS
BOOKSHOP AND EDITORIAL: 2482 TELEGRAPH,
BERKELEY CA., 94704
DISTRIBUTION: 2010 SEVENTH STREET, BERKELEY CA., 94710

FIRST PUBLISHED BY THE BUDDHIST SOCIETY 1935
SECOND IMPRESSION 1935
THIRD IMPRESSION 1937
FOURTH IMPRESSION 1938
FIFTH IMPRESSION 1940
SECOND (WAR) EDITION 1941
REPRINTED, 1943, 1947, 1948

PUBLISHED BY JOHN M WATKINS 1953
REPRINTED 1959

THIRD EDITION RE-SET PUBLISHED 1968
BY VINCENT STUART & JOHN M WATKINS LTD
45 LOWER BELGRAVE STREET
LONDON SW1

PRINTED AND BOUND IN GREAT BRITAIN BY
W & J MACKAY & CO LTD
CHATHAM KENT

This book is published in the Clear Light series dedicated to
W. Y. Evans-Wentz. The series is under the joint editorship
of Samuel Bercholz and Michael Fagan

SBN 7224 0040 3

Preface

To Third (Revised) Edition

IT IS now some thirty five years since I began to draft the material which was published by the Buddhist Society in 1935 as *Concentration and Meditation*, and I am asked by Mr Geoffrey Watkins who, at his father's famous shop in Cecil Court, sold the first copies, to make what corrections I wish for a third edition. He has helped me greatly in this task.

The genesis of the book explains one feature of it. In the early thirties there was a sudden spate of books on 'mind-development' of every kind which had one aim in common, to enable the practitioner to score off his rivals, in business, love or social climbing, to show off his alleged new powers and, generally speaking, to inflate his ego at the expense of those about him.

But there is a law as old as man to the effect that he who acquires the least advantage over his fellow men by the development of his own indwelling faculties must use them solely for the advantage of those fellow men, and never for himself alone. The law is utterly impersonal, and the penalty for disobedience is at least the loss of powers gained and, if the wrong course be pursued, what seems to be a shrivelling up of the mind which makes the sufferer the pity of his friends. One cannot therefore over-estimate the importance of right motive in any attempt at spiritual development. Hence the emphasis upon it throughout this manual, and indeed it was largely written to this end. It is therefore of interest—and as a Buddhist I do not believe in coincidence—that at a time when meditation is once more in the public mind a new edition of this work should be prepared and published. It certainly seems as timely now as it was in 1935.

My name appears as author, and in fact I drafted the material, section by section, for consideration at weekly meetings of the small society then known as the Buddhist Lodge. All present at each meeting had their say and many a point was carefully debated. I am therefore grateful to those unknown persons who helped to produce the book which finally appeared.

As I said in the Preface to the first edition, "For various reasons few detailed references have been given to books from which quotation has been made. Many of these have appeared in various editions, making accurate reference cumbersome, and space has been at all times limited. Moreover, the compilers in no way claim such extracts as authority in support of their own views, for they recognise no authority in matters spiritual save the intuition of the individual. Where, however, an idea is well expressed by another writer, his or her words have been used in addition to our own, while a generous use of quotation serves to show that the views put forward by the publishers are held by an ever-extending range of thoughtful minds."

"The book has been written for a hypothetical enquirer who is interested, yet knows nothing of the subject. Considerable space has therefore been devoted to the preliminary questions of right motive and the like, without which, in the opinion of the compilers, no such manual should be published. The book is compiled as a progressive course of mind-development, and it is hoped that a general reading of the manual, followed by a consistent and sincere attempt to apply its principles, will enable the average student, without danger to mind or body, to develop his spiritual qualities to the point when he is ready for that expert guidance without which it is so hard to tread the final stages to Enlightenment."

No knowledge of Buddhism is needed for an understanding of the principles herein explained, but as it is written with an emphasis on Buddhist ways of thought it will be the better understood after reading some general text-book on Buddhism. If I mention my own Pelican *Buddhism* (1951) it is only because it was prepared in somewhat the same way, and having sold steadily since publication it presumably serves its purpose.

There are now many books on meditation, but at the Buddhist Society we still discriminate between those which never mention the word motive and those which take the same view as ourselves about its fundamental necessity. The better type covers a wide field, from the Theravada school of Ceylon and Thailand, where the full system was written down some two thousand years ago, to the methods of Tibetan and Zen Buddhism both of which, however, have been in existence for over a thousand years. Yet no such work makes the distinction I deem so important, between Concentration, the controlled development of the mind as a precision instrument of no spiritual significance, and Meditation, the right use of it to spiritual as distinct from merely material ends.

Meditation is of course no new-comer to the West.

Christian communities have used it from time immemorial, and whether called prayer, meditation or silent communion its purpose was ever the same, the union— the Buddhist would say re-union—of the individual with the Universal Mind. That this has a thousand names is of no consequence. It remains forever the Namelessness, and when the dewdrop in full consciousness slips into the Shining Sea for a single 'moment of no-time' it needs no name for that supernal experience.

All that comes from the East is but a variety of methods new to the West, some of service to the Western mind and some which those with great experience hold to be quite unsuitable. There are no short-cuts to enlightenment. This is no place to make distinctions by name but from the Buddhist point of view two principles may be constantly borne in mind.

No true master of meditation will take one penny for his teaching.

No true master makes any claim, or allows any claim to be made on his behalf, to abnormal powers or achievement.

In order to improve the current edition I re-read every word of it, and was interested to note how little I wished to change. If I have grown in wisdom in these thirty-five years I have only developed my understanding of these eternal principles, and I humbly proffer this new edition as a guide which, rightly used, may help the reader to obey the final words of the All-Enlightened One "Work out your own salvation, with diligence."

Contents

The Importance of Right Motive—Self-
development or Service—Meditation and
Prayer—The Nature of Self—The Power
of Thought

PART ONE
Concentration

Definition of Terms—Dangers and Safe-
guards—Further Preliminary Observations

Concentration: General—The Value of Self-
recollection—Concentration: Particular Ex-
ercises—Time and Times—Place—Posture—
Relaxation—Breathing—Begin—An
Object or an Idea—Difficulties—Intruding
Thoughts

On a Physical Object—On Counting the
Breaths—On Watching Thoughts—On
Visualisation—On Colour—Summary of
Part One

PART TWO
Lower Meditation

Concentration and Meditation—The Purpose
of Meditation—The Results of Meditation—
Meditation: General and Particular—Choice

PART FOUR
Contemplation

Introduction

MOST OF the great religions and philosophies have stressed the importance of mind-development, but none so much as Buddhism, wherein it is regarded not merely as the principal occupation of the more enlightened student, but as an integral part of the daily life of the humblest follower of the All-Enlightened One. This attitude is based on common sense, for it is obvious that only in a fully developed and purified mind can the fires of anger, lust and illusion be stilled, and the cause of suffering destroyed. The very system of thought we know in the West as Buddhism is based on the supreme enlightenment gained by the Buddha in meditation; how else, then, shall we attain the same enlightenment if we do not follow in the self-same way?

In order to appreciate the importance of meditation in the Buddhist life one has only to consider the best known summaries of the Buddha's teaching as given by himself. 'Dana, Sila, Bhavana,' for example, is often given as such a summary. First comes Dana, universal charity, then Sila, strict morality, and thirdly, in progressive importance, Bhavana, mind-development. Again, "Cease to do evil; learn to do good; cleanse your own heart; this is the religion of the Buddhas." Note that so soon as ethical control is well established the "cleansing of the heart" must follow as the next step to the Goal. It is true that in one sense the various steps must be trodden simultaneously. One need not wait for ethical perfection before beginning to meditate, for it is only in meditation that the necessary wisdom and strength will be released for the task of self-purification. At the same time, it is well to consider these steps in the order given by the Buddha, for only when the preliminary stages are well in hand will the full benefits of meditation be obtained.

All this applies in particular to a still more famous summary of the Buddhist way of life, the Noble Eightfold Path, whose steps are frequently described as falling into three main groups. First, under right views and aspirations comes Right Knowledge; secondly, under right speech, action and livelihood comes Right Action, and finally, under the last three stages, usually translated as right effort, concentration and meditation, comes Right Mind-development. It seems clear, therefore, that meditation, using the term to summarize the last three stages of the Path, is not merely an integral part of Buddhism, but the very climax of its other doctines, laws and practices. Through this alone perfection lies; through this alone can one with patient toil unveil the Buddha light within. The field of mind-development, in brief, lies between the man of average culture and his further spiritual development as a bridge between mere worldly perfection, however gilded the shackles of Samsara, and the inner world of Reality where, on the threshold of Nirvana, he sees for the first time the true nature of the illusion left behind.

The Importance of Right Motive.

"Prepare thyself, for thou wilt have to travel on alone. The Teacher can but point the way." The cleansing of the heart is no light task, and as these words from *The*

Voice of the Silence show, it is a long and lonely road. It must needs be difficult, for the untrained stallions of the mind must be brought under control, and the littlest 'fond offence' brought out into the light and slain to rise no more. There are dangers on the Way, and those who succumb to them. As is pointed out in W. Q. Judge's *Culture of Concentration*, "Immense fields of investigation and experiment have to be traversed; dangers unthought of and forces unknown are to be met; and all must be overcome, for in this battle there is no quarter asked or given." The prize, however, is worth it all, to free oneself from the tyranny of earthly limitations, and with a soul that "lends its ear to every cry of pain, like as the lotus bares its heart to drink the morning sun," to join that unseen Brotherhood whose spiritual wisdom forms the guardian wall about humanity. Only with some such motive, however dimly formulated in the mind, is it wise to begin the practice of mind-development. Knowledge, and the power which knowledge confers, is a neutral force, becoming good or evil according as it is applied. Rightly used it is the high road to perfection; abused, and it can create a hell past human imagining. Between the two extremes of pure benevolence and absolute selfishness lie a variety of motives, all of which must sooner or later be eradicated from the mind. There is the desire to gain a superiority over one's fellows, either in one's own esteem or in actual competition in worldly affairs; there is the desire to find an escape from the monotony of daily duty or, more often in the case of women, a relief from the tedium of a purposeless existence; or again there may be a desire to experiment in some new 'stunt' with which to amuse oneself and one's equally ineffective friends. All these are so many ways of prostituting a sacred faculty, the abuse of which is the essence of 'black' magic and a long step on the road to spiritual death. There is only one right motive for mind-development, an understanding of the nature and purpose of man's evolution, and the will to hasten that evolution in order that all life may be the sooner brought to enlightenment.

Wherefore let every student pause, and consider well before embarking on this final science, this final stage of the ascent towards the Goal. Let him before he seeks the Changeless be certain that he wearies of the world of change, and longs with a yearning past denial to find and win Reality. Some reach this stage by an all too intimate acquaintance with the truth of suffering; some by an intellectual understanding of the illusory nature of phenomena and the will to discover the Noumenon which lies behind; others again are impelled by the rising call of pure compassion to dedicate their lives to lessening by just so much that "mighty sea of sorrow formed of the tears of men." These only may be certain that they enter the Path with proper motive, for those alone in whom the white flame of compassion is alight past all extinguishing appreciate that "to live to benefit mankind is the first step," and therefore lend an ear at all times to the voice of Compassion when it whispers: "Can there be bliss when all that lives must suffer? Shalt thou be saved and hear the whole world cry?"

There is no compromise when once the Path is entered. Once the feet are turned towards enlightenment the heart's attraction to the world is left behind. To move too soon is to intensify unduly the strain of rival attractions. Therefore let the mind and heart be single in purpose before the journey is undertaken, and let the motive above all be pure. That the practice of meditation tends to remove the fetters of suffering by raising the consciousness to a level above its sway is the testimony of all who practise it, but this is not the motive which will lead one to the Goal. Choose the way for its own sake before the life is entered. Right motive is always impersonal, an impersonal turning of the will towards the removal of all suffering, without undue attention to one's own, and an effort to uncover within each form of life that 'Essence of Mind,' which, as the *Sutra of Hui Neng* points out, 'is intrinsically pure'. "The Light is within thee," said the Egyptian Hierophants, "let the Light shine." To awaken in all forms of life this knowledge, and the way to realize it, is the aim of all who strive to follow in the footsteps of the All-Compassionate One.

Self-development or Service.

Do not be deceived by the false antithesis of self development and service, the Arhat and the Bodhisattva ideal. On the one hand, no man can be of service to others until he has attained some mastery of his own instruments; on the other hand, all self-development and purification is undertaken in vain so long as there remains thought of self. Once more, the wise man treads the Middle Way, for his life is a happy alternation between introversion and extraversion, between the subjective life

5

of meditation and the objective life of service. In service the subjective finds its liberation, yet that service will not be wise unless it is actuated from an understanding gained in the meditation hour.

Meditation and Prayer.

Most Westerners are born and bred in Christianity, and have in early years been habituated to the practice of prayer. The word has many meanings, varying with the spiritual development of the individual, but save in the true mystic its essence is always supplication to some external Being or Power. In meditation, however, there is no such element of importuning, of begging for what one has not. At the best the method of prayer is a yearning of the heart; meditation, on the other hand, reorientates the mind, thereby producing the knowledge by which all that is rightly wanted is acquired. The meditator does not ask for guidance, for he knows that a purified mind can call upon the Wisdom which dwells within; he does not crave for virtues, for he knows that in meditation he may and will acquire them; nor does he intercede for others when by his own unaided efforts he may assist them to the extent that their own *karma* will permit. In brief, prayer at its best is the approach of the heart, and produces the Mystic; meditation, with the wise service which accompanies it, produces the Knower. There is a point, however, where the two methods meet. If by prayer be meant 'a lifting onself to the level of the Eternal,' or even, if the desire be impersonal, 'the soul's sincere desire, uttered or unexpressed,' it ceases to be prayer in the ordinary sense of the term and rises to the

6

level of meditation. It is the element of supplication to an outside power, as distinct from a conscious union with the God within, which distinguishes the two.

The Nature of Self.

"Know thyself," said the Delphic Oracle. The way of meditation is the way of knowledge, and the aim of all such knowledge is to find and identify oneself with the Self within. It is therefore of extreme importance to possess some knowledge of the nature of Self and its vehicles, in order that the purpose and technique of meditation may be understood. The simplest analysis is that of St Paul into Body, Soul and Spirit, the first including the complex personality, the second all that is thought of as the Higher Self, and Spirit being as useful a term as any for what the Buddha called the "Unborn, Unoriginated, Uncreated and Unformed." These names have no validity in themselves; they are but "ways of speaking, definitions of everyday use," as the Buddha described his analysis of self to Potthapada the mendicant.

In considering these three divisons it is well to begin with That of which the others are the vehicles or forms. It is all too easy to think of man as having a soul or spirit, whereas in truth each man, each form of life, *is* in essence a spark of the Flame, 'a fragment of the Undivided clothed in the garments of illusion'. Hence the wealth of analogy and symbol used to describe evolution (the word itself means to unfold) as the revelation of an already existing splendour, a shedding of the veils which hide Reality. Not without reason does the East epitomise its wisdom in the phrase, "Become what you are."

This Spirit is no mere attribute. In India known as Atman it is the essential Man, yet in that it is but an indivisible aspect of the nameless All no man may claim that it is his alone. Hence the Buddhist doctrine of *anatta,* not Atta (Atman) designed to remove the illusion that there is any abiding principle in man, that there is in his composition any single attribute which distinguishes him eternally from other forms of life.

In brief, Spirit, like Nirvana, IS, and every form of life, or high or low, is but an everchanging manifestation of the eternally Unmanifest. The One however, manifests as the Many, and each spark of the Flame is wrapped in sheaths or bodies of increasing density. The most tenuous of its veils is *Buddhi,* the home of intuition, and this, together with *Manas,* mind, comprises what may be called the higher Self, as opposed to the composite personality whose final garment is the outward body of clay.

Each one of these bodies has a life and form of its own, the complex whole forming the Universe in miniature and therefore the key to all the Wisdom yet unknown. Unfortunately for our comfort, the desires of these vehicles are in the lower stages of evolution often incompatible with one another, and invariably inimical to the interests of the Self. The body has its own coarse physical desires; the emotional or passional nature craves for a strong vibration to give it stimulus; the rational or thinking mind cries out for its own food, and, like an unbroken stallion, fiercely resents the slightest attempt at control. This complex personality, the Buddhist *skandhas,* wages unceasing warfare with the higher Self for command of the whole, yet until this battle be finally won by the higher vehicles, this truer, slowly evolving Self can never fulfil its destiny and "merge the Ocean in the drop, the drop within the Ocean".

Most men are so immersed in the claims of the lower, selfish personality that they have lost all sense of that Golden Age of spiritual perfection to which they must eventually return, and for them the sense of warring duality, of unceasing inward strife has not begun. Sooner or later, however, the fight must be undertaken and fought to a finish on the battleground of the human heart. Here is the battle described in the *Bhagavad Gita,* and here the meeting ground of most of the poetry, legends, myths and allegories by which men learn of their spiritual heritage. Those who have no desire to fight must await the birth of courage. As the Master M. once wrote to A. P. Sinnett, "Life leads through many conflicts and trials, but he who does naught to conquer them can expect no triumphs." Nought else is of such absorbing interest, naught else has such a final value, for, as the words of the *Dhammapada* proclaim, "Though one should conquer in battle a thousand times a thousand men, he who conquers himself is the greatest warrior."

Yet, paradoxically enough, in this fight it is not the Self that fights. As is said in *The Voice of the Silence,* "The branches of the tree are shaken by the wind; the trunk remains unmoved." When the whole strength of the will is bent towards unselfish purposes the unruly lower vehicles are slowly brought into alignment, thus permitting an uninterrupted flow of Life from the highest to the lowest, making the man as a whole a channel of world enlightenment, a fountain of spiritual life to all mankind.

To produce this perfect alignment is one of the objects of meditation.

Now consciousness can function at any level on which it has an instrument. Most men live in their emotions or, at the best, the lower mind, but in meditation one raises the level of consciousness, reaching first the higher mind, the realm of abstract ideas and ideals, and then, at first in flashes of *satori,* as it is called in Zen Buddhism, and then continuously, the plane of intuition or Pure Knowledge, when thought has become unnecessary and the knower and the knowledge blend in one. From this point of view, the science of meditation may be called the culture of consciousness.

The subject of self must inevitably recur in this manual, but the foregoing will be sufficient as a background for the practical instruction which is to come. Applying the law of analogy, "as above, so below," the student will understand more and more of the nature of his own being, and thereby arrive the easier at the control of the lower vehicles. Yet let not over-study lead to an ego-centric attitude of mind. As is said in *Light on the Path,* the right motive for seeking self-knowledge is that which pertains to *knowledge* and not to *self.* "Self-knowledge is worth seeking by virtue of its being knowledge, and not by virtue of its pertaining to self."

The Power of Thought.

The West is not yet awake to the power of thought. Though conscious of the influence of strong 'personalities,' of mass suggestion by slogans and advertisement, and even of 'atmosphere' in certain places, it is left to a few advanced psychologists to appreciate the power of thought on health and character. Yet how many of these have reached an intellectual acceptance, much less a realization of the first verse of the *Dhammapada*: "All that we are is the result of what we have thought; it is founded on our thoughts, it is made up of our thoughts," and trimmed the sails of their research accordingly?

Yet so it is. All that we are and do is the result of what we have thought, and action, good or bad, may be described as precipitated thought. No single voluntary act can be performed without a preceding motion of the mind, however 'instantaneous'. From raising the foot to the planning of New Delhi, each act exists as a thought in the mind before that thought appears as an act.

Our behaviour, then, is the outcome of our mental processes, of what we are, but what we *are* at the moment depends on what we have *done* in the past. Thought, therefore, not only decides what we do, but what we are, whether that bundle of qualities be known as character, *karma* or the soul.

Now Buddhist philosophy has always taught, and modern science is gradually coming into line, that force and matter are interchangeable terms. There is neither an ultimate unit of matter nor of energy—the concepts are interchangeable. At one end of the scale, however, force is so little limited with matter that it may be thought of as 'pure' force, and at the other end matter is so dense that it may be regarded as motionless. Between these two extremes lies every degree of density of matter and purity of force. Now the level at which thought functions is higher than the highest level which the eye can see, yet thought is itself a form of matter as regards the medium in which it moves, though it may be regarded as force as regards its origin. But if the skilful hands of the potter can mould a lump of clay into the likeness of his thought, how much more does every thinker to some extent, and the trained thinker to a very great extent, mould the more tenuous matter of thought into definite shape as he decides at will. Hence the saying "thoughts are things," and hence the meaning of the word 'imagination,' which means image-building. These 'thought-forms,' however, not only exist in the imagination but are to be seen by a trained clairvoyant persisting in the thinker's mental atmosphere. The power of such thoughts varies, of course, with the intensity with which they were created, and their repetition. Most of them swiftly fade away; others remain, to have their inevitable reaction for good or bad on the mind which gave them birth. A thought of hatred against an individual will grow and grow until it becomes a cancer in the thinker's mind; a thought of love to an absent loved one stimulates the lover to still further love. But the effect of the thought-form does not end with its creation. Even as radio waves are picked up wherever a set is tuned-in to their wave-length, so the thoughts which each of us think each moment of the day go forth into the world to influence for good or bad each other human mind. Hence such phenomena as mob-psychology and telepathy, and hence the power of suggestion which is so little understood and so terribly abused.

Again, like attracts and breeds its like, and thoughts, whether good or bad, will collect and reproduce their kind. Hence the phenomena of temptation or 'conversion' as the case may be. As a man toys with the thought of stealing, so is he strengthening his movement towards theft, and as he ponders the foolishness of previous conduct, so is he strengthened in his resolve to turn away. As we think, so we become.

Mind-development, then, whether the meditation be turned without or within, is a subject worthy of most careful study and unceasing practice until the fruits themselves proclaim its value. That it is arduous, and even at times wearisome is not to be gain-said, but that it is ultimately necessary is the testimony of all the ages, and its reward is the end of suffering.

To those advanced in meditation the pages which follow will be of little value, but to those who are but entering the Path, or who, consumed with doubt, stand on the threshold irresolute, we offer the words of the Master K. H. to A. P. Sinnett: "We have one word for all aspirants—Try."

Part One

CONCENTRATION

CHAPTER ONE

Preliminary Observations

Definition of Terms.

MUCH UNNECESSARY confusion has been caused by the use of the same terms with widely different meanings. Let it therefore be noted that the following broad classification will be used throughout this work.

The process of mind-development falls into two main divisions, Concentration and Meditation. By the former we mean the preliminary exercises in one-pointedness of thought which must of necessity precede success in the latter, while Meditation will be considered under three sub-divisions. The first of these consists of early exercises in the right use of the instrument thus prepared, and will be described as Lower Meditation. Following this comes the realm of Higher Meditation, which in turn merges into Contemplation.

Our classification is therefore as follows:—

1. *Concentration.*

Before an instrument can be used it must be created. It is true that most men learn to concentrate on worldly affairs, but all such effort is directed towards the analysis, synthesis and comparison of facts and ideas, while the Concentration which is a necessary prelude to Meditation aims at unwavering focus on the chosen thing or idea to the exclusion of any other subject. Hence the need of strenuous and even wearisome exercises for developing the power of complete one-pointedness of thought upon the subject in hand, be it a pencil, a virtue, or a diagram imagined in the mind.

It will therefore be noted that Concentration, in the sense above described, has neither ethical nor spiritual value, and calls for no special time or place or posture for practising. The exercises correspond to those which a ballet dancer must use before the simplest dance can be performed, or to the earnest young pianist's scales, or the fencer's early lessons in precision of aim. Only when the executive instrument, be it the limb, the hands, or the machinery of thought, has been brought under control of the will, can the art itself be effectively developed.

2. *Lower Meditation.*

Under this heading come those mental exercises in which the newly-created instrument is first dedicated to useful work. It includes, for example, the meditation on the Bodies, on the fundamental doctrines of the Buddha's teaching, such as Karma, Rebirth, the oneness of life, the Three Fires, the Three Signs of Being, and early exercises in self-analysis. Needless to say, a perfect understanding of these subjects is a monopoly of a perfected mind, but a beginning is here made in the mastery of their true significance. Other subjects to be dealt with under this heading include the whole range of deliberate Character Building, the use of the four Brahma Viharas, and early steps in the deliberate raising of consciousness, which, as will be seen, is in a way the whole object of Higher Meditation.

The full range of this sub-division is therefore enormous, and it will take the average student many years and even lives to move beyond it. Within its compass lie the beginnings alike of mysticism and occultism, of Yoga and of Zen, for only in the later stages of Meditation are all these paths perceived as one Path, and all the goals perceived as One Reality.

3. *Higher Meditation.*

Stages two and three have no clear-cut dividing line, yet those who reach this level will at some great moment realize that a subtle yet tremendous change has taken place within. Henceforth they will be in the world and yet not of it; serving the world yet definitely liberated from its thrall. In meditation they will find that objects are transcended, and even names and definitions left behind. Here is a world whose scale of values is the essential nature of things and not their outer semblances, where for the first time the meditator is freed from the tyranny of forms. Henceforth the *karma* of the past may hold the student to sensuous and therefore valueless pursuits and interests, but his inner eyes will have seen the Vision glorious, and the hand of time alone will hold him from his heritage.

Under this sub-division fall the *Jhanas*, the stages of consciousness so fully described in the Buddhist Scriptures, and here belong the more difficult *koans* used so freely in Zen Buddhism. In this division, too, will be found the higher realms of mysticism, in which intense devotion blends with intense intellection in the understanding of pure abstractions and the relationship between them. Here is the meeting ground of mathematics and music, of metaphysics and pure mysticism, for here alone the limitations of form may be transcended, and the Essence of Mind perceived in all its purity.

4. *Contemplation.*

If there are comparatively few yet ready for higher Meditation, there are still fewer to whom the act of Contemplation is more than a nebulous ideal. This exquisite sense of union with Reality, of spiritual absorption into the very nature of one's ideal, though mentioned at greater length hereafter, can never be usefully treated in any text-book, for those who have reached such a level need no literature, and to those who have not so attained even the finest description would be almost meaningless.

Dangers and Safeguards.

There are those who hesitate to take up Meditation on account of its possible dangers to physical and mental health. Nothing, however, worth having can be attained without some risks, and an unfailing observance of the following three rules, together with the exercise of a little common-sense, will obviate these dangers and their unpleasant consequences.

1. *Seek wisdom and not powers.*

The necessity for purity of motive has already been emphasised, and it follows that any attempt to work for power or the development of psychic powers is extremely dangerous; nor is the development of abnormal powers any evidence of spiritual development. The 'power complex,' so easy to observe in one's neighbour's desire to dominate and impress his fellows, is latent in each one of us, and much that masquerades as altruism and a desire to help humanity will be found, on ruthless analysis in the meditation hour, to be nought but the will to self-aggrandisement. Spiritual pride is rightly regarded as one of the last of the Fetters to be broken, and whereas the premature development of powers inevitably serves to inflate one's egotism, the pursuit of wisdom will produce not merely power over other beings but power to control the lower self which otherwise would gain the mastery.

It is most unwise for an inexperienced student to concentrate on the psychic centres in the human body, however pure the motive, for concentration upon a centre stimulates its functioning, and as most people function primarily through the centres below the diaphragm, which govern sex and the lower emotions, their stimulation is clearly as unwise as it is dangerous. More men and women have been driven insane through a premature awakening of the forces latent in these centres than most students realize.

Nor will the pursuit of phenomena lead to enlightenment, for as Master M. once pointed out to A. P. Sinnett, "like the thirst for drink and opium, it grows with gratification. If you cannot be happy without phenomena you will never learn our philosophy. I tell you a profound truth in saying that if you but choose wisdom all other things will be added unto it—in time."

2. *Avoid 'stunts' and all excess.*

Once more the importance of pure motive is made evident, for any inclination to show off, or to boast of the length or results of one's meditation is a symptom that the snake of self is once more beginning to rear its head, to the detriment of true progress. It was from the depths of his wisdom that the Buddha sternly forbade his bhikkhus to make any such display, and even expelled from the Order those who were guilty of it. The same applies to excess. In the early stages of meditation one is developing a new set of (mental) muscles, and just as the athlete trains himself by slow yet progressive effort, so the spiritual athlete regards excess in any direction as a source, not of progress but of delay. Once more the touchstone of wise conduct is the Middle Way proclaimed by the All-Enlightened One.

3. *Never be negative.*

It is true that there is a form of spiritual passivity which is a proper stage of growth, but experience has shown that for the beginner the above rule should be carefully observed. Once more, the ideal is the Middle Way between an aggressively positive attitude of mind in which the noise of one's thought-machinery will drown the Voice which speaks only when the mind is stilled, and a negative, receptive attitude which places the whole personality at the mercy of any entity, human or sub-human, which cares to take possession. Obsession, complete or partial, permanent or temporary, is far more common than most students realize, but he who carefully cultivates a happy mean between the two extremes will be immune from every outside influence.

The ideal during meditation is to make the mind positive towards all outside interference, whether of intruding thoughts or actual entities, and yet be receptive to all higher influence coming from within. A little practice in this exercise will enable the student to achieve a happy combination of resistance and non-resistance, of positive and negative, in which all outside influence will be excluded, and yet the channels of inspiration be fully opened to the light within.

This being the unanimous advice of all who write on meditation, it is hardly necessary to point out the long delay in progress which any and every form of mediumship inevitably causes to the medium. As is well known to every student of Occultism, the adept and the medium are poles apart, and he who so far slips down the ladder of evolution as to give up his own self-mastery will spend many arduous lives in regaining his lost ground.

Further preliminary observations.

There are certain further rules or maxims to be borne in mind if meditation is to prove an entrance to the way of enlightenment and not merely an intellectual pastime.

1. *Do not begin unless you mean to continue.*

As already pointed out, meditation is not a hobby, and it is unwise to trifle with so serious a subject. As is said in the *Dhammapada,* "That which ought to be done, do with all vigour. A half-hearted follower of the Buddha spreads much evil around."

Progress is upward and must therefore be continuous, or the climber will slip back whence he came. At the same time progress must be gradual. "Just as, O bhikkhus, the mighty ocean deepens and slopes gradually down, not plunging by a sudden precipice, so in this Norm-

Discipline the training is gradual and there is no sudden penetration to insight." If progress seems to be slow, remember that lives of wrong habits of thought must be surmounted. To attempt to learn too fast will only lead to mental indigestion. As the Master M. once wrote to A. P. Sinnett, "Knowledge for the mind, like food for the body, is intended to feed and help to growth, but it requires to be well digested, and the more thoroughly and slowly the process is carried out the better both for body and mind." Patience is indeed a virtue, and a necessary quality in the would-be meditator. It is said that a Chinese craftsman thinks his life well spent if during it he creates one perfect masterpiece, and he who views the illusion of time through philosophic eyes will think a single life well spent if one small stage of the path be trodden thoroughly. Even if no single stage be perfectly accomplished, yet the student may take heart. As *The Voice of the Silence* says, "Learn that no efforts, not the smallest—whether in right or wrong direction—can vanish from the world of causes. E'en wasted smoke remains not traceless." So that the effort be continuous and sincere results are certain, however long delayed.

2. *Beware of self-congratulation.*

It is said that many a weakling can put up with failure but only a strong man can withstand success. When the first well-earned results of mental training begin to manifest, beware of the separative effect of self-conceit. "Self-gratulation, O Lanoo, is like unto a lofty tower up which a haughty fool has climbed. Thereon he sits in prideful solitude, and unperceived by any but himself." (*The*

Voice of the Silence.) All too soon a little success in the inner life will breed a sense of superiority over one's fellows, a sense of separation from those (apparently) less advanced upon the Way. Yet remember, as the writer of *Light on the Path* advises, that "great though the gulf may be between the good man and the sinner, it is greater between the good man and the man who has attained knowledge; it is immeasurable between the good man and the one on the threshold of divinity. Therefore be wary lest too soon you fancy yourself a thing apart from the mass. When you have found the beginning of the way the star of your soul will show its light, and by that light you will perceive how great is the darkness in which it burns."

3. *Beware of Guru-hunting.*

The Western world is filled with those who seek for 'Masters,' 'Gurus,' and other mysterious personages to lead them swiftly to the Goal. But there is no short cut to perfection, and the true Adepts will never help a student until, first, he has made all possible use of the materials at hand, and, secondly, he has by the purity of his life and aspiration shown himself worthy of their help. When that hour strikes, and not before, the Teacher will appear. Beware, then, of this craving for assistance, for it is born of laziness and conceit and is in turn the father of disappointment and delay.

4. *Ignore psychic experiences or the appearance of psychic powers.*

Meditation will sooner or later raise the consciousness

CONCENTRATION AND MEDITATION

to a level at which occasional and hazy glimpses will be obtained of the realm above the physical. This is the psychic world, filled only with the shadows and reflections of Reality, a world of illusion through which the seeker after truth must delicately pick his way. To one whose vision has hitherto been confined to the physical plane, anything super-physical is all too easily labelled 'spiritual,' and the visions, voices and 'messages' which fill the séance room can without difficulty impose themselves on a credulous audience as worthy of acceptance. Let not the student be fooled by their enchantment, nor by those who in all sincerity believe themselves the bearers of such 'messages.' There are in the West to-day a score of 'Adepts' and 'Messiahs,' many of whom genuinely believe the nonsense claimed on their behalf, yet a little commonsense would prick the bubble world of illusion in which they live. With a little less vanity they would wonder what qualities they had which caused them to be chosen as the Messenger, and they would be genuinely hurt on learning that it is a combination of vanity and a mediumistic make-up which lays them open to such psychic influence. The psychic world is filled with an immense variety of thought-forms built up by the human imagination, yet, radiant though they seem to untutored eyes in the starry light that surrounds all psychic visions, they are but the glamorous products of illusion.

The same considerations apply to the advent of psychic powers. Because the student occasionally becomes aware that he possesses senses which are super-physical, it only means that he has peeped through into the next plane of his being. Pass on, for here is the realm of illusion, and Reality lies far beyond. To waste one's precious time in cultivating psychic powers is to side-step from the Path of Self-Enlightenment. These powers will be useful at a later stage, but for the time being are best ignored.

5. *Learn to want to meditate.*

In other words, learn to direct desire. Unwilling work is badly done, and there is less waste of effort and a higher standard of workmanship in excercises carried out with the whole soul's will than in those which are the outcome of a habit forced on an unwilling mind. Until, therefore, the practice of meditation has become a joyous necessity, as mentioned in the next paragraph, do not be ashamed to give up a little time to achieving this attitude towards it. The ideal condition is what an engineer would describe as a clean drive through from the source of power to the point of application, in this case from the highest within one to the act itself. Internal friction only dissipates energy and reduces the output of useful work. The same applies to persuading others against their will to take up meditation before the desire to do so has been aroused. It is worth while studying the relation between will and desire. It is an ancient axiom that "behind will stands desire," for will is a colourless, impersonal force, and acts for good or evil as directed by desire. If the desires be rightly directed, the will becomes a powerful force for good in proportion as it is developed, that is, in propor-tion to the individual's ability to call upon the limitless reservoir of force which is the Universe. To one whose desires are purely altruistic this ability to "attach one's belt to the power-house of the Universe," as R. W. Trine calls it, will be indeed immeasurable, for just as the perfectly aligned machine will lead the thrust of the engine direct to its work, so the perfect alignment of will and desire will direct the Universal Will to the chosen end.

Modern psychology is slowly awakening to these ancient truths. A conflict between the desires of one's various vehicles will lead to a 'complex' more or less charged with emotion according to the strength of the desires, but "if thine eye be single the whole body will be full of light," and friction at an end. It is common knowledge that where there's a will there's a way, and if a man be pursuing his 'heart's desire,' he can accomplish seeming miracles. It is therefore wise to spend a little time considering the manifold desirability of mind-development, so that, once begun, the whole complex being of the student will move with singleness of aim towards the chosen goal.

There is no particular technique for bringing the desires into the required focus. No man digs for copper when he is finding gold, and honest comparison between the value of worldly pursuits and spiritual exercises will serve to concentrate the 'whole soul's will' in the direction indicated by the highest part of one. Desire is the motive force of all action, and is good or evil according as it strives for sensuous or spiritual ends. By thoughtfully comparing the permanent results achieved by meditation with the ephemeral pleasures gained by gratification of lower desires, the latter may be slowly sublimated into higher channels, until the strength once dissipated on lower pursuits is re-directed to spiritual ends.

There is another reason for this preliminary focus of desire, for it will be found in meditation that right desire excludes all alien thought. A man listening to his favourite symphony is oblivious to all distracting thoughts or happenings. In the same way a man whose sole desire is to gain what only meditation can produce will find the lesser attraction of intruding thought of no avail to draw him from his desire.

6. *Do not neglect existing duties.*

It has been said that meditation is first an effort, then a habit, and finally a joyous necessity. When the third stage comes, beware lest the discovery that it ranks in interest and value far ahead of earthly pursuits and happenings should lure one from the due performance of the daily round. Remember what H. P. Blavatsky says in *Practical Occultism*: "The immediate work, whatever it may be, has the abstract claim of duty, and its relative importance or non-importance is not to be considered at all." What else is the world around us but the soul's gymnasium? As the Master K.H. wrote to A. P. Sinnett, "Does it seem a small thing to you that the past year has been spent only in your 'family duties'? Nay, but what better cause for reward, what better discipline, than the daily and hourly performance of duty?". . . .

CHAPTER TWO

Concentration

"CONCENTRATION IS the narrowing of the field of attention in a manner and for a time determined by the will." These words of Ernest Wood in his book, *Raja Yoga*, explains the famous story told of Arjuna in Paramananda's *Concentration and Meditation*. "Once in ancient India there was a tournament held to test marksmanship in archery. A wooden fish was set up on a high pole and the eye of the fish was the target. One by one many valiant princes came and tried their skill, but in vain. Before each one shot his arrow the teacher asked him what he saw, and invariably all replied that they saw a fish on a pole at a great height with head, eyes, etc.; but Arjuna, as he took his aim, said: 'I see the eye of the fish,' and he was the only one who succeeded in hitting the mark."

The most helpful analogy is probably that of a searchlight. The factors which determine a searchlight's value are its power, its capacity for clear and unwavering focus, the size of the field thus clearly lighted, and the ease with which it can be focused where desired. The human equivalents of these factors will in like manner determine the value of the thought-machine as an instrument for meditation. All these factors are developed by the practice of concentration, the effect of sustained effort being an ever-increasing field of clear focus into which no extraneous subject may intrude.

Needless to say, proficiency in concentration is by no means easy to attain. As is written in the *Dhammapada*,

"Hard to control, unstable is the mind, ever in quest of delight," but, "good it is to subdue the mind, a mind controlled brings happiness." Like many other arts and sciences it is largely a matter of knack, and after long periods of seemingly fruitless efforts a semblance of proficiency will suddenly appear. The immediate results of such success will be a reduction in the usual wastage of thought energy, and consequently a greater reserve in hand. Then comes a sense of self-discovery, a dawning appreciation of the difference between the knower and the instrument of knowledge, the man and his various vehicles. From this in turn comes a deeper understanding of the meaning of self-mastery. The student finds new meaning in the famous passage in the *Dhammapada*, "Irrigators lead the water where they will; fletchers shape the arrow. Carpenters bend wood to their will; wise men shape themselves." Again, as thought is the father of action, control of thought leads to greater control on the physical plane. There is less waste of energy in useless movements of the hands and body, and therefore less fatigue. The natural reservoir of physical energy is thus allowed to accumulate until applied as definitely wanted and the general health is correspondingly improved. The next achievement is a greater co-ordination between the various planes of consciousness. Mind, emotion and action begin to function as one unit, and the waste of energy produced by 'worry' is replaced by a calm, deliberate effort to remove its cause.

So much for the credit side of the newly drawn-up balance sheet. As against this there is sometimes noted a curious sense of loss, a mental aridity and, as it were, an emotional vacuum. If this occurs, remember that it is a period of transition, in which the mind has been for the first time withdrawn from its habitual playground in the world of sense, and has not yet acclimatised itself to super-sensuous levels. More rare at this stage, but for the time being more unpleasant, is the experience of finding that life's difficulties, so far from growing less, seem to increase from the moment the new practice is begun. All who strive to hasten the slow march of evolution seem to call down upon themselves an increasing volume of their own past *karma*. If this be unpleasant to the personality it is to be welcomed by the essential man, for not until all *karma* is expended will he be able to press on to the ideal, the enlightenment of all humanity. On the other hand, there will be this compensating discovery, that in proportion as the student gains control of his vehicles so will his mental reaction to environment improve. Mere proficiency in concentration will of itself induce an improvement in character, and the student will begin to see that "facts are of no importance: what matters is their significance." Facts are facts, but it is for the individual to decide his reaction to them. As Epictetus pointed out, "If any man be unhappy, let him know that it is by reason of himself alone." The wise man will refuse to allow the changing face of circumstance to disturb his inner serenity.

Before proceeding to the practice of Concentration, let it be noted that there is a definite distinction between the development of the mind, which we are now considering, and the development of the emotions, to which we have devoted a chapter at a later stage. An apprecia-

tion of this distinction will provide an answer to the
charge that concentration is 'cold' and 'dull', and remind
the student that emotions are not suitable subjects for
concentration of the mind. As subjects for Lower Meditation, they are, of course, of value, but they are not fit
subjects for the acquisition of one-pointedness of thought.

CONCENTRATION: GENERAL

The subject of Concentration falls into two divisions,
General and Particular, the former consisting of the cultivation of an habitual mode of thought, and the latter
comprising the special exercises by which this quality of
mind is developed. Too much stress is laid in text-books
on the latter, and far too little on the need for cultivating
the right attitude of mind each hour of the day. As
Annie Besant wrote in her *Introduction to Yoga*, "Many
sit down for meditation and wonder why they do not
succeed. How can you suppose that half an hour of meditation and twenty-three and a half hours of scattering of
thought throughout the day and night will enable you to
concentrate during the half-hour? You have undone
during the day and night what you did in the morning,
as Penelope unravelled the web she wove," Unless the
whole day be spent in applying the lesson learnt in the
morning's exercise no progress will be made. Indeed,
there comes a time when the special exercises are given
up. A student writes from a Zen monastery in Japan: "As
one progresses further, meditation on one's *koan* continues through all one's waking hours and even, I think,
during one's sleep. The most advanced monks are given
practically no time for formal sitting, and yet they must

go (to the Abbot) for *koan* interview as many times as the young monks who spend the larger part of their waking hours in formal meditation. (When) meditation becomes a habit of mind, the formal side is discarded as much as possible."

The following suggestions may help in the cultivation of this attitude of mind:

1. *Get Physically Fit and Remain So.*

Remember that even in the highest meditation, consciousness must function through the physical brain, and unless the body is fit the brain will never function to the best of its ability. Physical fitness is not easy to acquire or maintain under modern conditions of living, but a little thought in acquiring the maximum of sunshine and fresh air, sufficient sleep, and the maximum purity of food will be well repaid. More than one aspirant to Yoga has pointed out that no good results can be obtained in a 'dirty' body, that is to say, one which, however clean without, is badly regulated within. Hence the saying, "the key to Yoga lies in the lower bowel," and certainly a lavish use of pure water, inside as well as out, goes far towards acquiring and maintaining a healthy physical instrument.

Having got the body fit, learn to dominate it. Treat it as the animal it is, considerately yet firmly, and train it in obedience with exercises in physical control. Learn to distinguish *its* desires from your own. *You* do not crave for tobacco, sweet-meats, comfort, warmth, or perfume. Let your body learn this fact by giving up, at least for a specified time, one 'fond offence,' be it cigarettes or coffee, silk underclothes or that extra ten minutes in bed. In the same way cultivate a philosophical indifference to the bumps and bruises of daily life, and refuse to listen to the body's perpetual plea for indulgence in its physical desires.

2. *Concentrate on the Task in Hand*

"The trivial round, the common task will furnish all we need to ask" of opportunity to develop a constant one-pointedness of mind. As a student wrote from the wisdom of experience, "Before one can meditate one must learn to concentrate; otherwise one will be possessed with the will and the inspiration, but lack the necessary third ingredient, technique. Begin by letting the whole of your day become an exercise in concentration, making each action to be done the one thing then worth doing. First say to yourself: 'I am now going to concentrate for (say) an hour on doing *this*, and let all other matters stand aside. This I shall do without thought of self, but because it is the right thing to be done.' Then forget all about the need to concentrate and get on with the job, whether it be the passing of an examination, the drafting of a document or the cleaning of a room." In order to accumulate the energy for this sustained effort, strive to eliminate all idle and purposeless activity, whether mental emotional or physical. In the ideal, every thought and act should have a purpose behind it, and be deliberately dedicated to a useful end. Mention has already been made of the need to curb unnecessary physical movements and mannerisms; the same applies to thought and feeling. Long periods of time are wasted in idle day-dreaming, or the useless harping upon some trivial fact or circumstance, and the same applies to indulgence in emotion without its corresponding thought and action. To pander to one's emotional craving for stimulus may afford one a pleasant 'kick,' but only adds to the difficulties of ultimate self-mastery. By ceasing to dissipate one's energies so lavishly on things of no importance there will be left in hand a larger capacity for organising the daily round in such a way that the maximum of useful work is accomplished in the minimum of time. It is proverbial that the busiest man finds it easiest to fit in something more, and an effectively ordered time-table, combined with a wise use of available energy, will enable the would-be meditator to find both the time and energy for this greatest of all exercises.

But Life for ever swings like a pendulum between the Pairs of Opposites. As the sequence of day and night, so is the alternation of work and rest, and it is in these minutes of comparative repose that the difference appears between the trained and the untrained student of mind-development. The beginner allows his energy to drain away in idle conversation or mental rambling, in vague revision of past experiences or anxiety over events as yet unborn, or in a thousand other wasteful ways for which, were he spending gold instead of mental energy, he would be hailed as a reckless spendthrift to be avoided by all prudent men. The wise man, however, learns the value of the smallest opportunity, and uses these otherwise idle moments to some useful end. Students of concentration practise a useful exercise, while those who have reached the stage of meditation keep a phrase in the mind to be mentally 'chewed over,' or carry in the pocket one of the many booklets of spiritual wisdom from which to gather nourishment for the self within. When it is appreciated, for example, that not only have thousands read, and even learnt by heart, Sir Edwin Arnold's *The Light of Asia* by this means, but that Sir Edwin actually wrote the greater part of it on scraps of paper in such odd moments of the day, some idea will be gained of the value to which these 'unforgiving minutes' may be put.

But, it may be argued, if every spare moment is used in such activity, what of the need for occasional repose? Only experience will prove the paradox that such a habit, so far from leading to further exhaustion, actually reinvigorates the mind. Again, once such a habit is formed, it will be found that the mind, when otherwise unoccupied, will tend to revert automatically to the central theme or phrase, and by thus filling the day with a succession of 'spiritual moments', the student will find his thought machinery being trained to an attitude of habitual concentration, on a worldly problem if so ordered, if not, on a theme of more permanent value to the inner man.

Even when the time comes for a well-earned rest it will be found advisable either to bring the mind to rest on a subject of value and interest, or else to learn how to suspend all mental activity. Far too little thought is given to the art of relaxation, yet never has it been more necessary than in these days of ceaseless dissipation of energy. Remember that recreation ought to be, as the word implies, a re-creation, and not a further expenditure of energy in useless pursuits. The study of newspapers, for instance, being the apotheosis of distraction, destroys the effect of exercises in concentration. Of far more recreative value is good literature, good music, the reading or writing of poetry, and, when feasible, the games of patience, jig-saw puzzles and the like which pleased an older generation, but which no longer satisfy the craze for speed and nervous excitement which characterises the present day. Beware, however, of emulating the amusing example of 'concentration' which once appeared in *Punch*, where a woman is shown sitting in an armchair and at the same time knitting, reading a book, listening to the wireless, rocking a cradle with her foot, and talking to her husband.

The alternative to such forms of relaxation as above described is to practise the art of complete relaxation of body and mind, ten minutes of which will be found to be more refreshing than hours of restless sleep. If circumstances permit lie full length on the floor; if not, on a couch or even in a chair. Loosen any tight clothing, then relax each portion of the body deliberately and consciously; then close the eyes and visualise utter darkness. Feel yourself floating in a silent void, and deliberately empty the mind of every thought or feeling by imagining such a condition as Swinburne's "Only a sleep eternal in an eternal night." Even five minutes of this exercise, once the knack is acquired, will produce an abundance of fresh energy and a clean-swept and invigorated mind.

3. *Clarify Every Issue and be Master of each Act.*

It is an astonishing fact that very few people think, though many think they do. Indeed modern psychology has proved that the majority of people bring into play a very small percentage of their total mental capacity.

Thinking is a process which has to be learnt like any other art or science, and it is to be regretted that so much time is given in our schools to the acquisition of knowledge and so little to the digestion and right use of such knowledge when acquired. But the material of thought is two-fold, facts and ideas, and how many human beings are capable of originating, considering and expressing an idea? The answer, if honest, would make painful reading, for the majority of men are unaware that they possess the machinery of thought. In most cases they behave as if their actions were the automatic reflex of an outside stimulus, a response so immediate that reason has no time in which to interfere.

The perfect man, before committing himself to any action, would ask himself, and insist on knowing truthfully, *why* he was about to act in the way proposed. This sounds an impossible ideal, but it is a most effective exercise in concentration. Until you get into the habit of knowing how and why an action is to be performed you cannot concentrate the whole of your faculties on doing it efficiently. An extension of this practice, the meditation on right motive, will be mentioned later; for the moment it is sufficient to note the need of being the master of each thought-process and action from its inception to its end. Let there be no more of that unworthy excuse for foolish action, "I did not think." The damage done, if any, will be none the less for being caused by thoughtlessness, and the *karmic* results will be the same.

When the act is complete, decide whether or not you wish to remember it. Many men pride themselves on a marvellous memory; others are just as proud of the ability to forget. Why carry about through life a tremendous burden of old memories? Let those of value be stored in clear-cut detail; for the rest, let every act be performed impersonally, and with full deliberation, then relegated to the mind's waste paper basket.

4. *Control your Reaction to Mass Opinion and Emotion.*

Arising from the need to be master of each thought and act comes the more subtle art of distinguishing between your own and outside thought. Ask yourself, when any thought impels you towards action, "Is it mine? Is it truly my own considered opinion, or is it merely an undigested reflection of the views of the morning paper, or the general opinion at the club?" In these days of a popular Press it is hard to form and keep one's own opinions, especially if they happen to run counter to popular prejudice. Many a man, for example, on the outbreak of war, is swept off his feet by cleverly worded appeals to the mass-consciousness, and truly believes that the patriotic nonsense poured into the public ear is his own considered views, while few are the women who are free from the dictates of a 'fashion' which may not please or even suit them, but which in the end they adopt under the delusion that it is their own considered choice.

Hence the need for a discriminating watch upon incoming thought, a mental filter through which no opinions alien to one's better nature can force their way. If such were a common practice there would be less unkindly and destructive gossip spread abroad through the medium of minds not one in ten of which believes the stories thus retailed.

In the same way the wise man will attempt to control his emotional reactions. More will be said of this when we come to consider the Meditation on the Bodies; for the moment it is sufficient to point out the need for controlling one's reflection of mass emotion whether of anger, praise or fear. Because our friends, or the Press, or even the nation at large decide to revile some person's or some other nation's character or behaviour, must we concur? The wise man decides his own reaction, if any, to all circumstances and thinks and feels and acts accordingly.

The Value of Self-recollection

These practices, if honestly pursued, will lead in time to the birth of a faculty which is best described as self-recollection. This complex quality, one of the distinguishing marks of spirituality, is nowhere better exemplified than in Buddhism. The Buddha laid great stress upon it. Asked for the meaning of the self-possession he so sternly advocated, he answered: "And how, brethren, is a brother self-possessed? Herein, brethren, a brother, both in his going forth and in his home-returning acts composedly. In looking forward and in looking back he acts composedly. In bending or stretching arm or body he acts composedly. In eating, drinking, chewing, swallowing, in relieving nature's needs, in going, standing, sitting, sleeping, waking, speaking, keeping silence, he acts composedly. That, brethren, is how a brother is self-possessed." Such a dignified, dispassionate inner poise must rouse the respectful admiration of all who strive towards self-mastery, yet it is but the outcome of a faith-

41

ful building into character of the hints and suggestions above set out.

As he begins to attain some measure of self-mastery, the student remembers that all that exists is the product of thought, and finds his centre of interest moving back from the visible world of effects to the inner world of causes. Even at this early stage, he begins to feel the rise and fall of the tide of world affairs, and to come into contact with those who know how "to watch, to dare and to be silent." No longer is he merely a puppet controlled by mass opinion, but in an increasing measure a co-worker with the forces of nature, moving intelligently towards the same beneficent end. When such a day arrives it will be well once more to examine the motives prompting further efforts, for know that it is the heart of wisdom which advises that "unless each step in inner growth finds corresponding expression in service to mankind the student treads a dangerous path, and works in vain."

CONCENTRATION: PARTICULAR EXERCISES

As already explained, there comes a time when special exercises carried out at special times of the day may be discarded, but for most of us for a long while the regular habit at a fixed time and place is helpful to progress, and the following suggestions may be useful during the periods so set aside:—

Time and Times

For obvious reasons morning is better than evening. In the first place, the earth currents are waxing up to noon, and waning from noon to midnight. To meditate at night is better than not to meditate at all, but when the earth forces are so negative extra caution is needed against adopting a negative attitude of mind. This is unlikely to happen in Concentration, but as Concentration is merely preliminary to Meditation, the same daily period should be used all through. There are other reasons for letting the chosen period begin the day. The brain is at its freshest after a night's sleep, and the manifold vibrations of the daily round have not yet "stirred the pools of thought". Again, to some extent in Concentration, and far more in Meditation, it will be found that if one begins the day by focussing the attention on the 'things that matter,' the whole outlook of the day's work will be brought into proper perspective. Many students both begin and end the day with such a period, and some find time to add a few more minutes in the middle of the day. There is high value in keeping the moment of noon as a period of self-recollection, for noon is the pinnacle of day, and countless groups and spiritual societies choose this moment for linking up in thought with the forces of good throughout the world. In the East the three best periods for meditation are given as dawn, noon and sunset. If dawn be impracticable and sunset difficult to ascertain, noon at least is easy to keep, and is the most powerful moment of all.

But whatever time or times be chosen, let them be regular. The mind, like the body, works best in a settled routine. When a single day's practice is omitted, three or four days' effort may be needed to make up the loss. It is true that there will come a time when the very habits thus made must be discarded, but the wise man does not scorn such adventitious aids until he has learnt to do without them. Such mental discipline by the use of unvarying habit is like the scaffolding erected round a growing building. When the building is complete, the scaffolding is taken away; until that time it is a necessary means to an end. Better, then, five minutes once a day and every day, than fifteen minutes twice or thrice a day when you feel like it.

No rules can be usefully laid down for the length of any exercises, whether in Concentration or Meditation, but all experienced teachers agree that it should at first be short. Fifteen minutes is cited as quite sufficient for the first twelve months, and even five minutes' strenuous effort, if regularly practised, will achieve remarkable results. Above all, err on the side of brevity. The humblest attempt at Concentration causes a hitherto unexperienced stimulation of the nerve centres of the brain, and over-stimulation may lead to serious trouble. Begin, then, with a very brief period, and let it be increased as comfort and experience dictate. After all, it is the quality rather than the quantity of effort that produces the qualities desired.

If at first it seems strangely difficult to 'find time' for these regular periods, however short, remember that you have definitely decided that there is nothing of greater or even equal importance in the daily programme and, secondly, that there are twenty four hours in every day. Careful thought, firm resolution, and a little tactful re-arrangement of the day's routine will always enable the genuine student to choose and keep at least one daily period, and once this is well established, further thought will find time for more and more.

PLACE AND POSTURE

Place

It matters little where the exercises are carried out, so that the chosen place be free from disturbance and always the same. When climate and mode of life permit it is better to meditate in the open than indoors, but for town-dwellers the privacy of one's bedroom is probably the best; those who can keep a small room in the house as a silence room are fortunate indeed.

Posture

Any position will do for concentration, though it is easier while seated in a cathedral than strap-hanging in an underground railway. For meditation, however, there are at least three requirements to be satisfied, and for reasons already explained it is best to acquire the right habits of time and posture from the very beginning. Choose, then, a position which keeps the head and spine erect, and bodily circuit closed, and the whole body at once poised and alert yet relaxed and comfortable. If an upright, unsupported back can be maintained with comfort, so much the better; if not, let the shoulders lightly rest against a support such as the wall, with a small cushion in the hollow of the back. The head should be held erect or drooping a little forward, as in the attitude of most Buddhist images. The eyes should be closed or fixed through half-closed lids on a chosen object. Either is equally effective for meditation, but the former is better for the eyes, a prolonged stare being apt to strain the optic nerve. The hands should be folded in the lap. Whether the body be seated cross-legged on a low seat or couch or upright in a chair is entirely for the student to decide. Comfort is the first necessity in order that the very existence of the body may be forgotten with the minimum delay. If a chair be used, let the feet be crossed, for this will serve the same purpose as crossed legs. The purpose of thus closing the circuit is to eliminate wastage of the energy generated during meditation, and in order that the positive and negative forces of the body may the more easily find their equilibrium.

Some students prefer to meditate while walking. It is true that monastic cloisters were built for this purpose, but it is doubtful if the same complete abstraction from the physical plane can be obtained in a moving body as in one deliberately stilled into the maximum repose compatible with waking consciousness. Here again, however, the student must make his own decision, and "work out his own salvation, with diligence".

Relaxation.

Having chosen the most convenient posture, make sure that no single muscle is in undue tension, for the body can never be forgotten while cramp or the desire to fidget intervene. Strive to imitate the glorious serenity of pose exhibited in every Buddhist figure. Too often in the moment of greatest concentration the body will follow suit. Tension between the eyebrows, a grim set of the jaw, an unconscious hunching of the shoulders or tensing of the hands, all these are familiar scenes to every teacher, but are habits to be dropped as soon as possible. Learn to dissociate the physical and mental functions. The car-driver may use the analogy of putting his engine (the mind) out of gear with the vehicle (the body). In order to

46

acquire this ease of posture, move the body about from the hips while deliberately relaxing every muscle, especially those of the shoulders and neck. When the body has finally come to rest it should have reached the stage when it has been 'poised, relaxed and forgotten.'

Breathing.

Now learn to breathe. Much has been written on this subject, and it may be considered from four points of view. First, as a means of quietening the body; secondly, as an actual subject of concentration; thirdly, as a form of yoga for the development of one's inner powers, and fourthly, in the course of the meditation on the 'bodies'. At the moment we are only concerned with the first, but even at this stage serious warning must be given which applies to the subject as a whole. As the Master K. H. wrote to A. P. Sinnett, injudicious practice in breath-control may "open wide the door to influences from the wrong quarter," and render one almost "impermeable to those from the right." In the absence of bodily purity and great experience the practice of special breathing may be very dangerous. It is in no way conducive to spiritual development, but has much to do with the psychic development which students at an early stage should best avoid. It is all too easy in one's ignorance to awaken forces over which one has no control yet which, when awakened, will place the student at the mercy of obsessing entities. For beginners, the safest and therefore, wisest course is merely to take half a dozen slow, deep breaths in order to induce physical repose, and to awaken the brain to its maximum functioning.

47

Begin.

Having settled these preliminary matters, take heart of courage and begin. Be not surprised that a whole paragraph is given to this little word, for many find it the hardest of all to apply. For every dozen persons who study mind-development there is but one who crosses the bridge dividing theory from practice, and there is much wisdom in the saying that the path to perfection has only two rules—Begin, and then Continue. Of what avail is it to take a ticket for a journey if one does not travel in the train, and why buy food and prepare it if it is not to be eaten? Herein lies the difference between knowledge and wisdom, for wisdom is born of the experience gained by knowledge applied. No great Teacher of men ever spoke as a theorist; each and all gave forth the message of their own experience. Take warning, then, and read no further in this book unless you intend to practise the science therein set out, for knowledge breeds responsibility, and knowledge unapplied, like undigested food, is a cause of suffering. Those who do read on must summon the will, direct it with the force of right desire, and strive to illumine the path with the light within, remembering that though a thousand difficulties will present themselves they are but aspects of the same implacable enemy—self.

Begin each period of concentration with an act of will. Formulate a firm intention in the mind and announce it to yourself. "I am now going to concentrate for so many minutes, and during that time I have interest in nothing else." If worldly matters are hovering on the margin of the mind deal with them rapidly, and definitely lay them aside as one might chain up a fractious puppy until it was time to take it for a walk. In the same way deal with each desire that threatens the mind's serenity.

Now choose the programme of work to be carried out. It is important to have this carefully drawn up, in order to save time during the concentration period and to eliminate the tendency to wander from subject to subject as the whim of the moment decides.

There is no one method of concentration suitable to all, for it has been said, "The Path is one for all, the means must vary with the Pilgrim," and again, "The ways to the Goal are as many as the lives of men." Allowance must be made for different types of mentality. Students are either predominantly intellectual or devotional, imaginative or practical, impetuous or leisurely, and must choose their method of work accordingly, either by following the line of least resistance, or by deliberately working to develop an aspect of themselves at the time comparatively unevolved.

But whatever method be chosen, let it be tried out faithfully before changing it for something else. Have faith in your own considered judgement, and even if 'results' are for a long time invisible carry on patiently, remembering that all experience is useful, and that before the ideal method is discovered a certain amount of trial and error must intervene.

An Object or an Idea.

Writers on the subject are divided on the relative value of taking as the subject of one's early studies a physical object or an idea, but strictly speaking it is a misuse of words to speak of "concentrating" on an idea. The process of such consideration is more accurately described as meditation, for an idea, to be of value, must be mentally assimilated, and this process is quite different from the purely objective exercises comprised under the term concentration. Nor is this a mere verbal quibble. In choosing a subject for concentration it is important to bear in mind exactly what one is trying to do. The searchlight of consciousness when directed to a given field of attention has, as it were, two qualities, extension and intensity. When playing on a distant landscape, for example, the light may either be diffused over a whole village or concentrated on a church tower, and the intensity of the light will vary with the extension of the field of view. As the whole object of concentration is to learn to focus the attention on a single point and to hold it there at will, it follows that the more simple the object chosen the more intense will be the concentration upon it. Even apart from these logical considerations, experience has shown that until one's mental power is considerably developed, the field of truly concentrated attention is very limited, and such an expansive object as a pure abstraction is beyond the range of the beginner.

Experience and logic are therefore agreed that a physical object is the wisest focus for first efforts in concentration, and the student is advised to attempt simple exercises before passing to more difficult, because more abstract realms.

Difficulties.

But whatever the subject chosen, difficulties will soon

arise, and it may be as well to consider them before passing to a series of specimen exercises.

1. *Increased restlessness.*

"The universal complaint which comes from those who are beginning to practise concentration is that the very attempt to concentrate results in a greater restlessness of the mind. To some extent this is true, for the law of action and reaction works here as everywhere, and the pressure put on the mind causes a corresponding reaction." Annie Besant, who devotes a whole chapter to 'Obstacles to Concentration' in her work *Thought Power*, goes on to point out that the increased restlessness is largely illusory. "So long as a man is yielding to every movement of the mind he does not realize its continual activity and restlessness; but when he steadies himself, when he ceases to move, then he feels the ceaseless motion of the mind he has hitherto obeyed." Each of the several vehicles through which consciousness functions has a collective life of its own, and the thought-machine, which for inumerable lives has never known obedience, naturally resents the first attempts at mastery. Like a young and spirited colt it has to be 'broken in'. For the first time the student definitely challenges his own mind, a foretaste of the later battle described in *The Voice of the Silence*: "The Mind is the great Slayer of the Real. Let the Disciple slay the Slayer." Picture the experienced trainer with an unbroken colt, patiently holding the rope while the furious animal plunges vainly in its efforts to be free, and remember that sooner or later the colt must learn to gallop, walk or be motionless at the dictates of the rider's will.

2. *Other difficulties.*

With divers other difficulties we have already dealt, but they will constantly recur. An impatience at the absence of 'results' is a symptom of wrong motive, while a host of unpleasant results such as headaches, insomnia, or irritability are symptoms of over-stimulation, to be cured by instantly reducing the duration of one's exercises. In the same way any attempt at 'guru-hunting' must be sternly repressed. The initial stages of this great enterprise must be mastered alone, and it is unwise to imagine that a little success entitles one to notice from those more advanced upon the way. Never forget that spiritual pride is the last of the Fetters to be broken, and that this hydra-headed monster will raise its head at every stage of the path.

Reference has already been made to the puzzling increase in misfortune which so frequently confronts the beginner. Yet remember that all *karma* is the result of actions which are definitely and irrevocably past, and that until these results are finally worked out you will be of limited use to humanity. The fruits of evil *karma* cheerfully borne can be made a source of spiritual strength, and so prepare one for the 'vortex of probation' into which all genuine efforts at self-development inevitably lead.

3. *Intruding thoughts.*

Of far greater difficulty is the problem of how best to deal with intruding thoughts. Whether the object chosen be a box of matches or a colour, a diagram or the process of breathing, a thousand other thoughts, either induced by the object under review or totally unconnected with it, will force themselves into the field of vision and try to lead the mind astray. Should one repress them, ignore them or deal with them?—for these seem to be the three alternatives.

Do not repress them.

There is great danger in using the will to repress or drive away intruding thoughts, for the result is analogous to stopping the circulation and is apt to react on the brain. Experienced teachers find that this is the cause of much of the fatigue of which students at times complain. It is an axiom of all mechanics, whether physical or spiritual, never to oppose one force with another when a less extravagant expenditure of energy will achieve the same result. It is far wiser to adopt the universal laws whose outward expression may be seen in the science of Judo by which the line of force of one's opponent's effort is skilfully avoided and then turned to his own undoing.

Few can ignore them.

For most students the advice to ignore intruding thoughts is to beg the question. The man who *can* ignore them has no need to consider how to deal with them, for they are never permitted to enter his field of consciousness, while those who find that they do intrude have proved their inability to ignore them. So long as they are merely hovering on the margin of the mind one may, by directing the 'whole soul's will' towards the chosen object, hold all alien thoughts at bay, but once the intruding thought has secured one's most unwilling attention it can no longer be ignored, and the student must needs consider the various methods of dealing with these unwelcome visitors.

Deal with them.

As already pointed out, uninvited thoughts are either those which, by a process of thought association, rapidly lead the attention a long way away from its chosen theme, or are quite unconnected with it, the former being far easier to control.

To take a simple example, one may begin to concentrate on an orange. Before one is aware of it, the mind has leapt from orange to fruit in general, from fruit to the need of buying some for lunch, from this to the theatre which the people coming to lunch are taking one to see, from this to tickets one promised to pick up on the way, and thence the best way of arriving at the theatre and the proper time to leave the house in order to get there in time. With a start you realize how far you have travelled from the orange, but instead of returning direct to the orange and beginning again, force the attention to travel back the way it came. From planning times and routes return to tickets, and thence to visitors, lunch, fruit and the need for it, and so back to the orange sitting in front of you. This habit of thought recalling is a valuable exercise in itself, and much may be learnt from it.

More difficult to handle is the slow procession of unconnected thoughts which wanders through the mind, each one clamouring for attention to the exclusion of all else. In dealing with these it is imperative to remain severely objective, refusing to yield to the least emotional

reaction of annoyance at the intrusion, or of like or dislike, fear or desire in relation to the intruding idea. In
other words, remain severely impersonal, as an observer
who feels no interest in the thoughts or their significance.
Adopt the principle, "Examine them, exhaust them and
let them go." Here is a practical application of the natural
law exemplified in the science of Judo. To resist these
invaders is waste of precious energy, while to examine
them calmly and impersonally as they pass through the
mind is to get rid of them with the minimum waste of
energy or time. Hence the Chinese saying: "Let thoughts
arise within your mind without repressing them and without being carried away by them. Let not the passing
thought be annihilated, and let not a passing thought rise
up again." Severely aloof from the slow procession,
remain an impersonal and impassive spectator of mental
processes. Refuse to let the mind become identified with
these unwanted strangers, for they are but products of the
mind and as such impermanent and fundamentally unreal.

A little patience in this point of view will not only
reduce the distractive power of such alien thoughts, but
reduce to a minimum those which have power to distract
at all. If some particular problem persistently recurs to the
point of inconvenience, adopt the late Dr Ernest Wood's
advice and "pause to give it a moment's consideration.
Say to it: 'Come, don't interrupt me now. I will attend to
you at five o'clock this afternoon,' and keep the appoint-
ment and think it *out*. If it still persists, consider
whether it has to do with a matter which is in your power
or not. If it is in your power decide to do something to
settle it. If you have done all that you can, or if it is not in

your power to settle it, decide finally that it has no concern with you and you will think of it no more." Needless to say, this advice may usefully be followed far beyond the realms of daily concentration, and applies to all the problems of life which arise and challenge us. If the intruding matter be something you have just remembered, or which you wish to consider at greater length hereafter, pause to make a pencilled note of it, and then return to your chosen theme. Such habits need not be scorned by the beginner, and may be abandoned when the need for them has gone.

In any event let patience be your watchword, and not irritation. Rome was not built in a day, nor the faculty of concentration, and sooner or later persistent effort will be crowned with due reward.

CHAPTER THREE

Exercises in Concentration

THESE EXERCISES are merely a selection, and every student is advised to seek for or invent as many more. The list which follows is devised merely to suggest the vast field of possibilities, the actual exercise used being of far less importance than the method of using it and the purpose for which it is used.

1. *On a physical Object.*

The object chosen is of little importance so long as it is small and simple, such as an orange, a matchbox, a watch or a pencil. Such objects as a lamp or the point of a burning joss-stick are sometimes mentioned in text-books, but concentration on a point of light is apt to lead to self-hypnosis, and is therefore to be avoided.

Place or choose an object a few feet away and then, when all preliminaries are over, deliberately focus the searchlight of the mind upon it. Begin by thinking *about* it, and then, at a later stage, narrow down the focus of mental vision and think only *of* it, or *at* it. The difference is subtle yet considerable. In thinking *about* a matchbox one may consider its various parts and properties, its sides and top, its colour and shape, its substance and surface, but of thinking *of* it these products of analysis die away and there remains in the whole field of consciousness one object only, the matchbox. Hence the need for an object at once small and simple, one which can be visualized without difficulty as a whole. Simple diagrams, boldly drawn, will be found suitable, but care must be taken to keep the mind upon the design, and to prevent it passing by a natural transference of thought to elaborations and variations of the diagram, or to the abstraction which it represents.

Realize frankly that this exercise is only a mental gymnastic and as such has neither moral nor intellectual value, then see if you can do it for sixty seconds without the slightest deviation of thought. If you cannot, face the humiliating fact with honesty, and so appreciate, it may be for the first time, the gulf which lies between you and even elementary thought-control. When you can really carry out this exercise for three whole minutes continuously there will be time enough to move on to the next. Note that in this exercise the only one of the five senses used is sight, but as Ernest Wood points out, "complete seclusion and quietude are not possible even for a short time. This, however, does not matter much if you train your senses to ignore the records of the sense organs. When we are deeply engrossed in a book we may be unaware that birds are singing outside, or that the clock is ticking on the mantel-shelf. It is not that the ear does not respond to the sounds, but that the senses are turned away from the sense organs." Hence the value of this exercise in learning to control one's sense reaction to outside stimuli. Decide that only the vibration of light, affecting the organs of sight, shall claim your attention, and refuse to heed all others.

At a later stage more subjective sense stimuli will claim the attention. A tickle in the foot or the sound of one's own heart beating will tend to distract the mind.

These may themselves be chosen later on as subjects for concentration, but unless so chosen they must be, like the ticking of the clock, to the best of one's ability ignored.

It will be found that this exercise is not only a useful, but a necessary training for those in subjective visualization, which will be described later. It has been pointed out that one who has perfected this training can at any time turn his attention to any object in daily life with which he has to deal, and grasp the whole of it at once without effort. What is more, he can carry away with him a mental image which he can consider or describe at his leisure later on. In the same way this training leads to greater ability in memorization, as also the ability to erase from the mind a matter which is finished.

2. *On counting the breaths.*

Concentration on a physical object implies keeping the eyes open, and is purely objective. The next exercise is intermediate between objective and subjective concentration, it being immaterial whether the eyes are kept open or shut. The breaths to be counted must be full and deep, and as breath is the very essence of physical life, it will be well to learn first how to control one's breathing.

Text-books and the methods of the several schools differ on the relative value of various forms of breathing, that is to say whether one merely breathes in and out, or breathes in, holds the breath in, and then breathes out and holds the breath out before once more breathing in. Even in the latter exercise there are a variety of rhythms, the most favoured being so many in, half that amount held in, the same number out, e.g., breathe in eight, hold four, breathe out eight and hold out four. The great point is to fill the body with air to its maximum capacity and then to empty it as far as possible. The incidental result after a few weeks will be a remarkable sense of poise and power and a material improvement in physical health. At the same time care must be taken that the body is at all times in a position of comfort and ease, and never tense or strained.

In learning to breathe fully the following description of the Zen method as taught to a European student in Japan may be followed with safety and benefit. "Begin to breathe, slowly and deeply, the lips closed, both inhalation and exhalation being taken through the nose. As you inhale you will distend and raise the chest, pull the abdomen in and in so doing raise the diaphragm. When you exhale you will depress the chest, distend the abdomen, and push the diaphragm down. This way of breathing is exactly the opposite to most methods, for when you are inhaling you will think of pulling up as far as possible the wall of the diaphragm, and when you are exhaling, of pushing it down and out against the solar plexus. As you continue, and do not have to concentrate too much on the muscular control of the breathing, you will find that you can press the diaphragm still further down until the final pressure seems to come just below the navel. Note that it is to the exhaled breath that one puts one's attention. The exhaled breath should be considerably slower than the inhaled breath, the exhaled breath and the downward pressure continuing so long that the inhalation is a reflex action from the exhalation."

Having just learnt to breathe, begin counting the breaths, thinking of nothing save the counting. It sounds easy until you try it, but an exercise which has been used by the Buddhist Sangha for unnumbered centuries, and is used to-day throughout the Buddhist world, is worthy of much respect, and will be found far harder than it seems. To quote again from the same Zen student in Japan, "Begin to count the breaths up to ten. Then begin again at one and continue the counting up to ten indefinitely. You will keep your mind on the breath count and on that alone. When other thoughts come in don't try to get rid of them, but just keep on counting and push them out of the way. A wilful attempt to keep away other thoughts only seems to make for more disturbance. Just keep patiently coming back to the counting. I found this exercise very difficult at first. Three hundred counts, that is, ten counted thirty times, is considered the goal to aim for, but these three hundred must be made without another thought of any kind coming in in the entire course of the practice." For beginners, it will probably be sufficient to attempt fifty counts with a perfectly concentrated mind, remembering that each of these breaths must be slow and complete. This exercise should be performed, if possible, in front of an open window.

3. *On watching thoughts.*

Assuming that by now the student has acquired the ability to concentrate upon one chosen object for a definite period, he may proceed to use the very intruding thoughts which at an earlier stage were such a nuisance. The first step is to develop towards them an

attitude entirely impersonal, thus laying the foundation for the removal of that selfishness which it is the
purpose of meditation to destroy. Ask them as they flow
through the mind, "Whose are you?" and when the
answer comes, as come it must, "Not yours," begin to
think of them impersonally, and merely note that the
thought of this or the desire for that is now arising in the
mind, is passing before the mind, is passing from the
mind, and watch the unceasing process calmly and dispassionately. Note how the thoughts flow past in an
unbroken succession, each the outcome of the last, but
only two being linked before one's mental vision at a
time. By such dispassionate examination of the flow of
thought it will become easier to control the stream of
unwanted visitors when desiring to concentrate upon
something else, but the danger of this exercise, if begun
too early, is that the mind, not yet sufficiently controlled,
will run after some attractive thought as a puppy following a stranger in the street. Hence the need, while per-
forming this exercise, of an active and fully attentive
mind which, while watching the flow of thoughts becomes
attached to none of them. At a later stage one may return
to this exercise and use it as a meditation on impermanence, on the nature of consciousness and the non-
existence of a personal self.

Allied to this exercise is another in which each
thought is deliberately followed backwards to its source.
By tracing these unwanted thoughts to their source one
is dragging each suppressed desire and emotion before
the bar of reason, where, in the light of cold analysis, it
may, if not too complex and deep-seated, be at once and

finally destroyed. It is unwise, however, to practise 'thinking backwards' with a view to remembering past lives. In the first place it is a waste of valuable time and energy, and secondly, by concentrating on past follies and unworthy actions, one tends to reproduce them before one's present consciousness, and so bring back to life what is best left unremembered. The present moment should have our full attention. We are in a sense, as the law of *karma* demonstrates, the creation of our own past actions, and we shall move the faster towards the goal by moving ever onwards than by pausing to look back.

4. *On Visualization.*

The power of forming clear-cut mental images is essential to progress in meditation, and the more thoroughly it is developed the easier it will be to perform the exercises described at a later stage.

Begin by placing in front of you some two-dimensional object, such as a simple diagram or design, and having considered it with complete one-pointedness of mind, close the eyes. Now create by the power of imagination, the image-building faculty of the mind, a mental reproduction of the object, or at least of its essential parts. Should any part of it be insufficiently clear, open the eyes and correct your observation and memory until the image and its original coincide. Then try the same exercise with a simple three-dimensional object, such as a matchbox, but see that the object chosen is neither too light in colour nor too dark. Without this precaution you may unwittingly increase your difficulties by reproducing on the retina of the eye an image of the object with the colours and light values reversed. This image, clearly seen, for example, by gazing at a window opening and then closing the eyes, may well be confused with the true mental image, which is entirely subjective, and should be an accurate reproduction of the original. At a later stage, if you wish to perfect your powers of observation and memory, practise the game immortalised in Kipling's *Kim*, in which one has, say, a minute in which to look at a trayful of small objects never seen before, and then, with eyes closed or back turned, must describe in detail the objects on the tray. This game, however, is primarily an exercise in accurate observation and memory, and here we are only concerned with the development of that concentrated attention which photographs upon the screen of memory the smallest detail in the chosen field of view.

Now turn your attention to the control of consciousness, the secret of which lies in learning to dissociate consciousness from the vehicle through which at the moment it happens to be functioning. Place before you an empty matchbox; form of it a mental duplicate in the plastic substance of thought, and begin to examine it from various points of view. Imagine yourself above it, looking down on it, or consider it from below. Then get inside it, and if this seems a curious proceeding, remember that though consciousness must use, in the sense of manifesting through, some form or vehicle, yet itself has none. It is therefore as feasible to imagine one's consciousness exactly filling a matchbox as a cathedral, the size of its usual vehicle, the physical body, being of no importance at all. There is much wisdom in some stories written for children, and when the heroine of *Alice in Wonderland* became larger or smaller according as she nibbled from this side or that of the toadstool on which sat the philosophic caterpillar, she was but experiencing what each student should discover and practise, albeit subconsciously for himself.

One of the most remarkable claims of Eastern adepts in mind development is that the mind contains, though as yet but rarely developed, all the faculties possessed by Western scientific instruments. It is said, for example, that a highly developed mind contains both microscopic and telescopic powers only limited by its lack of development, and all who have read accounts of the powers of consciousness exhibited by such Eastern yogis as are prepared to display their powers to Westerners will have no difficulty in believing that the true adept has astonishing powers indeed. These powers, however, lie far ahead of most of us, but the exercises above described for learning control of consciousness will prove a useful preparation for these more difficult mental adventures.

As the development of the exercise with the matchbox above set out, learn to move consciousness from point to point about a room or building. If at a lecture, for example, imagine yourself standing at the lecturer's side and look at the audience from his point of view. Another variation is to close one's eyes while travelling in a train or other vehicle, and imagine that one is travelling in the opposite direction. If these exercises seem trivial and foolish, the answer is that either you can do them or you cannot. If you cannot, do not despise them; if you can, you may pass from them without delay. Their value, apart from teaching one to concentrate, is that they tend to break up the narrow, egocentric attitude of mind which is the product of the illusion of individual consciousness, an illusion fatal to true mind-development.

Those who concentrate upon an imagined diagram may be annoyed to find how difficult it is to keep the image still, for some students find that it contracts and expands, or fades and reappears beyond the mind's control. Until this phenomenon has been mastered it may therefore be wiser to use words, in the sense of the letters composing them, or simple glyphs and symbols, though even here the image sometimes seems to have an impish life of its own. Once more let it be pointed out that the object chosen is of no importance, so that its image be kept clear cut and motionless before the mind.

5. *On Colour*.

This is really another exercise in visualization, but it deserves, together with its variations, a category to itself. In that the object visualized is formless, it is far more difficult than anything hitherto described, and complete success argues considerable development. It consists in flooding the field of mental vision with some primary colour, and then slowly moving through the various grades of mixture to some other primary colour. Suppose, for instance, that you wish to pass from blue to yellow. Close the eyes and visualize blue, not any blue *thing*, but blue. Now slowly infuse the blue with yellow so that it begins to show as a more greeny blue, not in patches, but simultaneously everwhere. Continue to make it greener and greener until the half-way point is reached, and you have a world of vivid green, remembering all the while that at the appearance of any green thing or form, or of any other thought than greenness you must begin again. Continue by making your green more yellow until it is more of a greeny yellow, and so through all gradations of colour until your world is a pure and brilliant yellow without taint or blemish of blue. Then, if you wish, reverse the process back through green to blue.

In the same way one may use the other sense for exercises in concentration. Take, for example, a note on the piano, and when it has fallen to silence continue it in the mind for as long as possible. At a later stage the note can be imagined from the first, and elaborations added. If you are musically trained, imagine an elaborate chord and try to hear its component factors separately. Resolve it into the minor key and back again, all the while keeping each note separately sounding in the inner ear. The sense of touch may be similarly employed, for one may imagine a sense of warmth increasing to great heat and then growing cool again. In the same way the senses of smell and taste may be utilized, the principle being the same, that the whole attention is focussed on the chosen sensation to the exclusion of any other sense reaction, subjective or objective, or any alien object or idea.

Summary

To summarize this portion of the book we would recall to mind the following propositions:

1. That until the mind has been thoroughly and patiently trained in concentration it is both useless and dangerous to attempt to meditate, useless because the student will lack the faculty of one-pointed thought

which is essential to successful meditation, dangerous because the application of uncontrolled and untrained energies to spiritual problems will all too easily result in moral and mental disturbances, reacting through bodily disorders on the physical plane.

2. That purity of motive is of paramount importance, for the slightest trace of selfishness and vanity is apt to grow with lightning speed and, like a pestilential weed, to strangle the flower of nascent spirituality.

3. That each man marches towards perfection on his own two feet. "Even Buddhas do but point the way." There is no such thing as vicarious progress. No reading of books or attending of lectures will avail as a substitute for personal effort. Forget not the Buddha's last injunction: "Work out your own salvation, with diligence."

4. That all that can be said or written on the subject of concentration may be summarized in three words: "Begin, and persevere."

Part Two

LOWER MEDITATION

CHAPTER FOUR

Lower Meditation

LET US assume that after many a promise made to yourself and broken, and many a genuine effort to begin which somehow failed, you have at last triumphantly begun; let us assume that after a series of doubts, delays and disappointments you have taught the unwilling mind obedience, and let us assume that after a period of wearisome and thankless toil some measure of efficiency in concentration has been won; what then? The answer is that when the searchlight of the mind is ready, and its beam become a sword of light obedient to the will, let it be used for the high purpose which engendered it. Around each one of us lies a tiny circle of light which we have wrested from the darkness of *avidya* (ignorance). Only in meditation can that circle of light be widened, and its brightness made a guiding beacon for those less fortunate. Here in this double purpose lies the goal of meditation, to increase one's own enlightenment, and to share it with the suffering millions of mankind.

Concentration and Meditation

Although there is no clear-cut dividing line between the habits and methods of concentration and meditation, yet the two are so distinct that it is well to bear the essential differences in mind. In the former the student is consciously controlling his instrument, and is aware of every mental effort, whether to keep out intruding thoughts or to visualize the object chosen; in the latter he no more thinks of the mechanics of concentration than a skilful driver thinks of the manifold processes which, when learning to drive, he found it so hard to master. Hereafter, once the object of meditation is chosen and the mental searchlight focussed where desired, the meditator must be able to assume that it will remain unaltered until switched off or re-directed by the will.

The second point to observe is that whereas concentration is a process, useful in daily life but having in itself no moral or spiritual significance, meditation produces a state of consciousness in which the spiritual point of view is alone of importance. If science be regarded as an expedition into the universe around us, meditation may be looked upon as a march within. Herein lies the essential difference between the laws and conditions pertaining to these two worlds. Knowledge concerning concentration may be openly taught for money, and no more reverence need be accorded such information than the equivalent knowledge about physical development. In meditation, however, the student enters another world, a realm in which, as only experience will make clear to him, all values are profoundly altered, and the relative importance of many of the 'pairs of opposites' reversed. Here motive becomes of paramount importance, and laws as yet unknown begin to operate. Henceforth it is forbidden absolutely, not merely to sell, but to use for personal ends the knowledge or powers obtained. To prostitute these powers to selfish ends not only dams the source from which they came, but causes untold suffering in lives to come.

Again, one may speak of one's experiences in concentration with any man; there is no need for reticence in this mental counterpart of 'physical jerks'. With meditation, however, new considerations apply. Here is the threshold to more spiritual levels of consciousness, and habits which will later become necessities may as well be formed at the start. It is unwise to discuss with strangers one's spiritual adventures unless it be in an attitude of mutual helpfulness. Sooner or later one must learn not only 'to know' and 'to dare,' but also 'to keep silent,' and it will be well to learn at once the value both of silence and occasional solitude.

There is a further price to pay, for it is a law of life that we must pay for everything, spiritual as well as material, sacrificing the lower for every gain in higher things. He who would learn to develop his inner faculties must pay the price of greater purity of life, lest morally he fall to the temptation of unworthy motive, and physically he be injured by spiritual forces flowing through a vehicle unable to accommodate them. If too fierce an electric current be passed through feeble or defective apparatus the latter will be shattered, and the electrical analogy applies to forces which are merely electricity on a very much higher plane. Henceforth there must be no excess of self-indulgence. Meat and other coarse forms of food impair the physical instrument's efficiency as a conductor of these forces, and alcohol is inimical to spiritual growth. Sexual over-indulgence, narcotics or drugs of every kind now become a serious hindrance, and at a later stage positively dangerous. On the other hand, physical aids to meditation become of definite value, though not as yet in any way necessary. It will be found increasingly helpful to keep to the same times every day, and if possible to use the same place or room. In the same way it becomes progressively more important to keep strict watch upon the tongue and those thoughtless habits of mind already proscribed on a previous page. Above all, the greatest care must be taken to exclude from the mind that most subtle of all vices, spiritual pride. Not without reason is it placed last but one in the list of the Ten Fetters which bind man to the Wheel of Becoming, for Ignorance alone can bind a man who has banished pride. It is easy to choose an ideal and begin to move towards it, but it is equally easy to slip into the habit of paying greater attention to the 'I' which is moving forward than to the ideal at which it is aimed. The wise man knows the wisdom of humility.

Hence the importance of constantly testing motives to make sure that the heights attained will not be the measure of one's fall, for self, like a sudden wind in mountain places, has hurled many a climber back to the bottom in the moment of his expected victory.

The intensification of the inner life will prove to the student still in need of proof how vast is the gulf which lies between the pseudo-meditation of idle day-dreams and the dynamic intensity which alone leads to success. The very strength of this newly-awakened force is apt, however, to rouse and bring to the surface the worst as well as the best in us. Unpleasant faults and failings long thought dead renew their menace, and before the mind can be made a conduit pipe for pure enlightenment, this refuse of past *karma* must be purged away. He is a bold man who imagines that a fault no longer active is therefore dead. From the deeps of experience does *The Voice of the Silence* advise: "Kill out desire, but if thou killest it take heed lest from the dead it should again arise." Evolution moves in upward spirals, and from time to time we reach the same point on a higher plane, only to find that vices long forgotten once more claim unwilling audience. The wise man, therefore, does not force the pace too much at the beginning but, like an experienced mountain climber, gives himself time to grow acclimatised at every stage of the ascent before rising to the next unconquered pinnacle.

The Purpose of Meditation.—What then is the purpose of Meditation? It is three-fold, to dominate the lower, separative self, to develop the mind's own higher faculties towards a vision of life's essential unity, and to unite this dual process in one continuous spiritual unfolding.

1. *To dominate the separated self.*

"I am not yet I am." In these few words lie hidden the secret and the paradox of man. Poetry, drama, myth and legend, each in their own way have attempted to portray this eternal struggle between man's higher and lower principles, and most that has yet been written on the subject of religion has little more to offer than so many methods by which the final conquest of the lower elements may be attained. That the task is infinitely difficult none denies—"Though one should conquer in battle a thousand times a thousand men, he who conquers himself is the greatest warrior." Yet all the religions of antiquity have spoken of salvation as the moment when the focus point of consciousness 'crosses the bridge' or 'passes through the gate' dividing the higher and lower aspects of our complex being, and he who has thus raised the level of his consciousness to a spiritual centre of gravity will bear witness to the bitter struggle which preceded victory. The actual conquest of the lower self pertains to the science of character-building rather than to meditation, but the spiritual trend of thought and moral self-control engendered by habitual meditation helps enormously in such a process, and may therefore be legitimately described as one of its principal aims.

2. *To develop higher faculties.*

These faculties are not to be confused with 'powers,' in the sense of the supernormal abilities of clairvoyance, psychometry and the like, many of which pertain to psychism rather than to spirituality. Rather they are the awakening of hitherto dormant aspects of the inner man, and are the result of the deliberate expansion of the field of consciousness which comes, at first spasmodically and as the result of effort, later with increasing ease and for longer periods. One may describe the process as the raising of the rate of the mind's vibration. Science is beginning to realize that Energy (or Spirit) and Matter are the two poles of the same primordial source, varying only in the rate of vibration at which they manifest. Most of us, for example, tend to focus our consciousness in the feelings or the concrete mind, thus limiting ourselves to the negative world of effects. Yet far above these levels lies the world of causes, and he who would learn to co-operate with the ordered processes of cosmic evolution, or 'becoming,' must rise of his own effort to the plane on which alone they may be understood.

It has been said that in the word expansion lies the secret of enlightenment, for only as the fetters of the personality are progressively transcended does man become that every-expanding 'moreness' which ultimately merges in the All. Hence Sir Edwin Arnold's phrase, "Forgoing self, the Universe grows 'I'," for it is far more correct to speak of the dewdrop becoming the Shining Sea than, as in Sir Edwin's famous stanza, slipping into it. It is indeed a paradox that as the limitations of narrow prejudice and personal desire are overcome, so does the inner man increase in spiritual magnitude.

3. *To align the higher and lower self.*

There are those who concentrate their energies on slaying selfishness and the faults and failings of the personality; there are those who ignore the claims of the lower self and strive to rise above its limitations by developing the synthetic and expansive vision of the higher mind. There is a third and equally important use for meditation, to fuse these two opposing aspects of the self into an undivided unity. There is in fact no essential difference between the two. When the stallions of desire are firmly harnessed to the driver's will there is no longer war between them, and in the perfect man there is no lack of harmony between his sovereign will and his various vehicles. This process of alignment is, however, most difficult, for at one stage of his evolution every student finds his higher and lower selves opposed to one another as for a fight to the finish, and in this final struggle no man can assist his brother to win the final victory. When some measure of selflessness has been achieved, it is time to begin incorporating into the higher self the subjugated lower principles, in order that the higher and lower no longer at war with one another, may learn to move towards enlightenment as a united whole. This effort at alignment, a harmonizing of the various vehicles of consciousness so that they form together a conduit pipe of spiritual force, is in a way the highest goal of meditation, for to the extent that the effort is successful does the individual cease to function as a separated entity and become 'a mere beneficent force in nature,' the very light of enlightenment.

The Results of Meditation

The results of meditation in its early stages are both negative and positive. On the one hand, by reducing the mind's reaction to outside stimulus the student acquires a hitherto undreamed-of equanimity; concurrently, he develops increasing understanding of human nature, his own included, with a corresponding increase in compassion for "that mighty sea of sorrow formed of the tears of men".

This calm serenity, the ability to be at all times and under all circumstances 'mindful and self-possessed,' has two aspects. On the one hand it implies an unruffled calm in the face of outward happenings; on the other hand, the mind becomes more and more a mirror to the light within. The East is rich in symbolism, and we read of the mind as likened to a pool whose surface, when ruffled by the winds of anger or desire, is unable to reflect the sun. Counselling A. P. Sinnett not to allow the serenity of his mind to be disturbed during the hours of his literary labours, the Master K.H. writes: "It is upon the serene and placid surface of the unruffled mind that the visions gathered from the invisible find a representation in the visible world." In other words, inspiration cannot work through a turbulent instrument, or, to change the analogy, the eye of wisdom cannot see clearly through the mists of emotion and desire.

This poise of mind, this "inner stillness and heart's quietude," begets an immense, unmoving dignity, from which in turn is born in others a profound respect for the one who displays it, with consequent enquiries as to the philosophy which gave it birth. There are many spurious substitutes, ranging from smug complacency to ponderous solemnity, both of which show the baseness of their metal by lacking that spiritual necessity, a sense of humour. True equanimity is unmistakable, for it combines with this air of having achieved a spiritual centre of gravity an inward joy, as of one who has glimpsed the illimitable happiness which springs from liberation from desire. It is a noble quality, and even the first beginnings of it are ample compensation for the long self-discipline involved.

If this serenity be in one sense negative, an absence of self-identification with circumstance, the second result is essentially positive, the ability to grasp and understand an ever-increasing range of human consciousness, both good and evil, and to perceive the world of causes behind the daily panorama of effects. Meditation upon those laws of harmony we know as *karma* will induce a progressive understanding of one's own and one's neighbour's actions, and the attitude of mind of which those actions are the effects. From such increasingly skilful diagnosis comes the desire to help, and a combination of this understanding and compassion only needs the addition of experience to qualify the student as a spiritual healer in the true sense of the term. Each virtue, however, has its own temptations, and an understanding of human nature is no excuse for interfering in other people's affairs. There is danger in another's duty, and unsolicited interference in another's problems may do more harm than good.

Meditation, General and Particular

Just as the practice of concentration is divided into a constant attitude of mind and definite exercises at special hours, so the particular exercises in meditation used in the special periods will be of little avail unless carried out all day. It would be possible to tabulate the general and particular application of meditation at each stage of progress, and with a little thought and the use of analogy the student can work out a table for himself. The need of correct posture in actual meditation, for example, works out during the rest of the day as the right care and use of the body as one's physical vehicle of consciousness. Again, breathing which in the special periods is deep, deliberate and, at a later stage, used for special purposes, should manifest for the rest of the day as full and rhythmic breathing able to be used, when so required, to calm undue agitation or to reduce fatigue. In the realm of motive, the detailed self-analysis of the morning or evening period will work out as an habitual 'self-recollection' as to the motives for each act, while the ability acquired in meditation of fusing one's consciousness with a chosen object is only a special application of the larger task of viewing life from a Universal point of view.

Choice of Method

Methods of concentration must vary with the needs of the individual, but all of them are directed to the same immediate end, control of the thought-processes. With meditation, however, the choice of method is infinitely greater, for the varying paths which open before each beginner may not reach the common goal for many lives. The goal of concentration is immediate and finite; the goal of meditation is ultimate and infinite.

Yet who can say that here and now he will begin? No student of the inner life can say when he first came to such a subject; if strongly attracted to it in this life, it stands to reason he was at least mildly attracted to it in lives gone by. It follows, then, that in this present life we can but make a fresh beginning, gathering the threads of past experience and once more striving to weave them into a preconceived design. The problem, therefore, is not so much what line of approach shall each of us adopt, as what is the path along which we are already travelling, in other words, the line of least resistance for our present needs? The paths are legion, yet each is an aspect of the Path. A classification of all known varieties would fill a volume, for male and female, East and West, mystic and occultist, introvert and extrovert all are examples of the 'pairs of opposites' of which both aspects must be experienced before we can tread the Middle Way.

Again, what is the relation between the mystic and the occultist? It has been said that the mystic seeks above all a realization of life's essential unity, and only when this is achieved does he return with 'the vision glorious' enshrined imperishably in his inmost consciousness. By striving for this sense of unity to the relative exclusion of all other interests, he mounts the ladder of spiritual progress leaving many steps untrod, but when, having achieved the mystic's consciousness, he concentrates his whole attention on the conquest of each plane of being, he does so with an uninterrupted vision of the Whole of which each is a part. The occultist, on the other hand, climbs step by step the ladder of his complex being until at the threshold of the highest he finds himself in the presence of his own Divinity, or Buddhahood.

Such are a few of the classifications in which each individual must find his own peculiar needs and difficulties. The goal is the same, a perfect balance of the best of each, and how one sets about the task of achieving it is for the individual to decide. No man is completely either of these complementary opposites, but most people tend to display in any one life a leaning towards one of them. Both are, of course, of equal value, so long as at all times one develops and displays a genuine tolerance for the opposite method and point of view.

It may be that some will find their type more easily in one of the branches of Yoga, such as the way of wisdom (*Jñana Yoga*), the way of spiritual devotion and beauty (*Bhakti Yoga*), or the way of action, or service to humanity

(*Karma Yoga*). The perfect man, of course, shows forth the qualities of all three methods of approach, but until we are perfect we needs must specialize, while striving at the same time to acquire the complementary virtues of the other paths.

New Difficulties

With meditation new difficulties will appear. In the first place, the very effort to control the lower self will produce by way of reaction a temporary increase in egotism, and a period will come when this illusory self will seem to stand as an objective obstacle in the path of progress. Be patient with this new phenomenon, for the illusion of a thousand lives is not removed in a day.

A more difficult problem, because entirely new, will be the claims of the intellect, which, with the antagonism displayed by every vehicle when it is sought for the first time to bring it under control, will fight for self-existence with an amazing variety of subtle wiles and unsound arguments. With an arrogance peculiar to itself it will strive to persuade the meditator that in this sphere alone lies truth, and it is all too noticeable that the West as a whole is a victim of this arrogance. Yet the intellect in itself is but a moulder of forms, and sooner or later consciousness must rise above the limitations which form implies. Hence the saying in *The Voice of the Silence,* "Mind is the great Slayer of the Real; let the Disciple slay the Slayer." To such an extent are most of us dominated by the intellect, or 'thought-machine,' that in the early stages of meditation we fail to appreciate how it is deceiving us. Many a student imagines, for example, that he is meditating upon his chosen subject, only to find on strict analysis that the real object of his meditation is "I am meditating upon so and so!"

Meditation with and without Seed

The arbitrary division of meditation into Lower and Higher, here made for convenience, corresponds to the meditation 'with and without seed' of other writers on the subject, the seed being the subject of meditation. Not until considerable experience has been gained in the former may the latter be carefully attempted, for abstract meditation tried too early is apt to produce a negative attitude of mind, with consequent discouragement, loss of concentration, and waste of time. The choice of the seed-thought, like the choice of method, is infinite in variety, and so long as the object be appropriate to the method its nature is immaterial. It is, however, advisable not to be too ambitious in the early stages, and to choose a positive rather than a negative point of view. If the subject be a moral one, for example, choose the value of a virtue rather than the demerits of a vice. In the same way it is wider to move ever forward into the future than, as it were, to move backwards with the eyes fixed in the past.

In order to ensure the continuance of this positive attitude of mind, avoid any form of self-hypnosis, whether induced physically by the use of mirrors or a spot of light, or more subtly by the repetition of words. Remember that the world of meditation is filled with hostile forces which, though merely the products of our own past *karma*, are far more dangerous and powerful than any worldly foe. Wherefore is the meditator described as being a warrior, using at times, it may be, strange methods of fighting, such as 'conquest by surrender,' but nevertheless at all times positive, dynamic, and possessed of 'iron determination and indomitable will'.

Preparation for Meditation

Time. If possible let the daily period begin the day. It stands to reason that at the end of a long day's happenings the mind is in a state of flux, whereas in the morning it is relatively quiet and therefore more easily raised to higher levels of consciousness. Again, if we start the day with a mind that is focussed on spiritual values, we shall live at any rate part of the day from a spiritual point of view, and once this habit is formed it is only a matter of time before the whole trend of our daily life is modelled upon the ideals of the meditation period.

Place. It will be found advisable to use, if possible, the same place every day, for the area chosen will be gradually tuned to the vibration of the meditator's mind. As such, it will become in time so sympathetic to his mode of thought that it will form, as it were, a garment of thought-substance to be assumed at will, thus saving the waste of energy of re-creating this atmosphere ever time. In this way the student will be able to begin his meditation each day at a comparatively high level, without having to build anew from the foundations every time he settles himself to meditate.

Whether or not an image or symbol is used depends very largely on whether the eyes are kept open or shut. If the latter, an image is superfluous; if the former, it may serve as a focus for the mind in the early stages, and by the power of suggestion induce an appropriate mental attitude.

The breathing should then be considered, full, rhythmic and deep in the preliminary exercises, becoming more and more shallow until in deep meditation it is almost unnoticeable. As will be described later, some students begin every period with a combination of deep breathing and 'passing through the bodies,' thus at the same time stilling the mind, emotions and physical vehicle, and leaving one free to function solely through the higher mind.

The Power of Stillness.

As the long process of self-development, of unceasingly 'becoming more,' begins to be seriously undertaken, the student will learn to rely to an ever increasing extent on his own reserves of strength and wisdom, in brief, to retire within. This does not, or should not imply moroseness, or even a lessening of good fellowship with friends and chance acquaintances, still less should it manifest as an egoistic self-sufficiency. Rather it is the product of an ever growing realization of life's unity, with an understanding that each unit of life has its roots in the common whole.

This double point of view, that in one's inner being lies all wisdom if only it can be brought through into the mind, and that the same wisdom lies hidden at the heart of every other aspect of the same life-unity, prepares the way for an understanding of the power of stillness. To some extent this may be experienced all the time, but for the beginner it is most easily found when deliberately sought, in quiet surroundings of natural beauty for those fortunate enough to live in or near the country, for the rest, where best they may. Here, in the 'secret places of the heart,' the student must learn to draw on the reservoir of his own potentialities, and to know that in his own inner being lie the answers to every spiritual problem, the strength to overcome all weakness, and the vision which will one day merge in self-enlightenment. Here, in the quiet hills of his own divinity, or Buddhahood, the happenings of daily life are seen for what they are, a series of effects whose causes lie in the mind now temporarily stilled, and here, in this inner quietude, the pilgrim, resting from his labours, may draw just so much nearer to his own ideal.

The Power of the Ideal.

All writers on the subject of spiritual development are agreed on the power of the ideal to draw one upwards to the goal. The faithful worship of a high ideal can overcome, as nothing else, the weariness which descends on all of us at times, and turn this depression into renewed enthusiasm. Be not afraid of the attitude of worship, for it is only when the object of worship is unworthy or untrue that it is a hindrance. A noble ideal, if firmly held and steadily pursued, is the most powerful agent for self-unfolding known to man. It acts both as a guiding star in the darkness of our imperfection, and as a model upon which to mould the plastic substance of our thoughts, and outward acts. The process of evolution is not merely an ever-becoming, it is an ever-becoming-More, and if the Most at which we aim be sufficiently definite we shall move the more swiftly towards its accomplishment.

CHAPTER FIVE

Objects of Meditation

THE PALI CANON mentions some forty subjects for
meditation, and there are, of course, many more used in
the various Mahayana Schools. A classified description of
the former will be found in Volume II of *The Path of
Purity*, being the *Visuddhimagga* of Buddhagosha, or in
Chapter IV of Warren's *Buddhism in Translations*,
while the whole range of Buddhist meditation is reviewed
in Tillyard's *Spiritual Exercises*. Generally speaking,
though it is difficult to generalize about such variety, the
forty subjects mentioned in the Pali Scriptures are
intended to subdue attachment to the senses, and to lead
the student to a conviction that all existence is but a
shadow of reality, this process being a necessary preliminary to a positive acquisition of true wisdom by the
development of the higher faculties. The whole series is
really summed up in the Four "Fundamentals of Atten-
tiveness," to wit, the Body, Sensations, Mind and the
Elements of Being. For this and other reasons the form of
meditation here called Meditation on the Bodies, which is
closely analogous, is placed at the head of the few main
divisions of meditation subjects which space permits us to
describe.

1. *Meditation on the Bodies.*

There are few persons of education who are not aware,
however dimly, that the physical body does not comprise
the totality of self, but before meditation can proceed

very far the student must not only free himself from the bondage of the visible body, but likewise remove the fetters of feeling and thought. Yet, as already explained, each of these vehicles of consciousness has a definite life of its own, and a great deal of effort will be required before they can be subdued to the will and used as a single complex instrument for the higher consciousness. To this end students are advised to begin at the beginning, and to meditate for a while upon each of the three vehicles of consciousness through which we contact respectively the physical, emotional and mental spheres of activity. When each has been separately considered as to its nature and special function in man's complex being, there will be time enough to begin using the meditation as a whole, which may be found at its simplest in Lazenby's *The Servant:*

> "I am not my physical body, but that which uses it.
> I am not my emotions, but that which controls them.
> I am not my mental images, but that which creates them."

The Physical Body

First learn to watch the body objectively, and study it as an entity having habits, desires, and even thoughts of its own. Note how at times it is restless for exercise and movement and at other times difficult to move. It wants food and drink. It desires warmth or coolness, sweet tastes, sweet scents, soft contacts for the skin. *You* do not want to wallow in a hot bath, but your body does. Thus three at least of the senses crave their own satisfaction, those of sight and sound being more in the nature of avenues to the mind. Having learnt this much about the body, drill yourself to a ceaseless memory of the difference between *its* desires and yours.

Control of the Senses

At this stage may be founded a greater control of one's sense reactions. As is written in the second chapter of the *Bhagavad Gita*, "He is confirmed in spiritual knowledge, when, like the tortoise, he can draw in all his senses and restrain them from their wonted purposes." A little practice in this will greatly facilitate meditation, both particular and general. Useful in learning to concentrate, it is an actual necessity in meditation, for energy which ever runs towards each fresh attraction, like the butterfly mind of a child, is not yet available for use in self-development. Keep watch, then, on these doorways of the mind, and remember that *you* are not interested in the manifold distractions of the outer world.

The Emotions

Having learnt to say, as a statement of realized fact,
"I am not my body, *I* am never ill,
  Nor restless, weary, fretful, ill at ease,"
tackle the emotional nature with the same reasoned thoroughness. Realize that *you* are never angry, jealous, frightened or depressed, and so begin that difficult task, dominion over mood. Emotions are not evil and need not be crushed out, but like uncultured savages these and others like them demand a constant supply of ever-changing vibration which is, of course, inimical to the mind's serenity. Learn, therefore, to dissociate yourself

from these emotions, and thus be in a better position to
control them. The danger to the mind is as great with
"good" as with "evil" emotions. Pleasure at success can
prove as unbalancing as depression at failure, and even
uncontrolled affection can do great harm. In this connection learn to use deep breathing as a method of
emotional control. Emotions react upon and function
through the nervous system, and rhythmic breathing
calms the nerves more effectively than any drugs.

The Mind

Having thoroughly appreciated that "*I* am not my
emotions, *I* do not feel," tackle a still more difficult
problem, the mind. This word covers in Western ter-
minology such a large section of man's being that it must
be further sub-divided, and for the purposes of this
meditation it is to be regarded as the 'thought-machine,'
the creator and user of concepts, whether useful or harm-
ful, borrowed or one's own. Here is the seat of *sakkayaditthi*, the 'heresy of separateness,' that is, the belief that
the separated personality is the real man, for it is a
characteristic of the 'lower mind' to cling to its own
importance and advancement, as distinct from the needs
and interests of other minds. Here is the seat of prejudice
and pride, and as most of us spend at least the greater
part of our lives at this level of consciousness, it is most
difficult to overcome. Begin by regarding this aspect of the
mind as the home of Hatred, Lust and Illusion, the
'three fires' of the Buddha's teaching, which burn in
every mind and hold one from enlightenment. The
hatred here described means all antipathy of thought, all

feeling of separation from other forms of life; desire includes ambition and all forms of covetousness, and by illusion is meant the countless bonds of ignorance which cause us to do evil for want of appreciating what is good. Watch the arising and passing away of thoughts as they come into the mind. Then notice the distinction between thinking *about* a subject and fusing one's consciousness with it so that one understands it, as it were, from inside; the former is a sign of the lower mind, the latter of the more intuitive or higher mind. Try to destroy the lower mind's inherent egotism by less use of the pronoun "I". Instead of saying "I am thinking a noble thought or a thought of hatred," say, "Here is a noble or an angry thought arising, developing and passing away." It is but a short step from this to a new attitude towards possessions, whether of goods and chattels or of knowledge and ideas. See that you possess them and not they you. There is an amusing description by a husband of his wife buying a hat: "They looked at one another for some time, her desire and the hat, and then the hat bought her." A little clear thinking will make plain that *I* do not own a suit of clothes or a car, still less do I own ideas. They are but appurtenances of my personality, and while in my possession are to be regarded in the same light as my body, as materials for wise and thoughtful use in the endless task of self and world enlightenment.

When each of these three divisions of the meditation on the bodies has been to some extent mastered, use them together as a deliberate raising of the level of consciousness from lower to higher, or finer instruments. At first one may use the analogy of rising through the bodies to a higher level, or of retiring inwards towards the centre of one's being through concentric circles of bodies, or again, of moving forward through realm after realm of matter towards a distant goal of universal consciousness. But whatever analogy is used there comes a time when the habitual vehicles of self-expression are transcended, and the student pauses at the threshold of a world unknown. Yet here before him lies Reality, though still enclosed in ever finer veils or vehicles of matter, and he must needs have courage who would woo enlightenment. In the latter stages of meditation on the mind one will have discovered that 'thoughts indeed are things,' and have learnt to handle concepts as a mason handles chiselled blocks of stone, building with them an ever nobler house of wisdom, but the time will come when concepts are transcended, and the student with a faith born of conviction leaps into the darkness, to land for the first time in a realm of consciousness in which the knower and the known, the meditator and the subject of his meditation blend in one. The meditation on the bodies is designed to produce as quickly as possible this state of mind, in which the limitations of space and time no longer hedge one in, and the mind is poised, as it were, in a sea of light. Hence the value of practising this exercise at the outset of one's attempts at meditation, and hence the habit of beginning every meditation with a rapid passage through the bodies in order to sever all connection with the outer world as swiftly as possible. From such a position of spiritual poise one may then turn the searchlight of one's intuition on whatever subject has been chosen as the task in hand.

2. *The Meditation on Things as they are*

Buddhism is a religion of knowledge, for its goal is Enlightenment. But before one can know one must want to know and those of whom this may be truly said are few indeed. Many are drawn to the study of spiritual wisdom because their intuition tells them it is true, yet on being faced with it they shrink away in fear. Sometimes the cause is an unwillingness to give up the selfish, lazy round of life which constitutes their principal existence; others, more active mentally, realize that the winds of truth will play havoc with the elaborate structure, built of second-hand belief and prejudice, in which their mind lies comfortably fettered, and fearing lest it fall in ruins, lack the courage or the energy to build anew. Yet no man sees the face of truth until he *wants* to see the face of truth 'with all the whole soul's will'. Study the truth, then, whether it seem to you pleasant or unpleasant, but do not force your understanding of it upon others.

The golden rule in practising this meditation is to learn to study things and ideas impersonally, without reference to their effect upon or relationship with oneself. Who can analyze dispassionately a matter which closely touches himself, for example the relative merits of his own and his neighbour's children, and who can accurately describe his house, his wife, his income or his future prospects without reference to what he hopes they will be, thinks they ought to be, or wishes they were? Aim at accurate, disinterested contemplation of things as they are, and consider your own relation to them, if any, afterwards. Then learn to extend this to examining yourself and all your actions in the same impersonal, dispassionate way.

This exercise involves the removal of a series of mental blinkers which prevent the majority of us seeing anything but what we want to see. In the first place we come to the examination of any object, whether the state of trade or a choice of diet, with a host of prejudices imposed upon us by early environment and education, and the views of the Press and of our friends. "What are the facts?" should be our constant query, for when these are truly ascertained there is time enough to consider what, if anything, is to be done about them.

Secondly, we are all too often blinded by the outer form. We dislike a man for the colour of his skin or a car for the colour of its paint. We approve of a book because it has nice large print, or of a friend because he has a house in the country for week-ends. Yet these are not the essential functions of these things, but accidents of form. Learn, then, to judge an object by its essential properties and functions, not by the outer form, for the same object may appear to a dozen different people in a dozen different ways.

A third type of obstacle to accurate mental vision is the name and label by which a thing is known, yet "a rose by any other name would smell as sweet," and a hat is a hat for all that it is called a hundred different names in a hundred different languages. We know that it is a virtue to call a spade a spade, yet all too often we imagine it is something different when called an agricultural implement. This form of blinker is still more noticeable in the world of thought. Certain doctrines are so old that they

must have borne a thousand different names in the course
of history, yet many still imagine that the truth within
them varies with the name. The doctrine of *karma*, for
example, is or is not true, but it is no more nor less true
because found in the Pali Scriptures, the New Testament
or the Daily Mail. Many students behave the same way
over those coloured boxes of thought we call religions.
Provided a man holds certain views and strives to live
accordingly, what does it matter if he calls himself a
Buddhist, Theosophist or Transcendental Theorist?
Conversely, the fact that a doctrine is labelled Buddhist,
or any other "-ist" does not make it any the more or less
true.

Finally, study all things in the light of the law of change.
What may have been true in 1900 is not necessarily true
to-day, for as yet we are unable to contact the absolute
truth, and the truth we succeed in finding is only relative
to ourselves. It is a commonplace that what is true for me
to-day may not be true for me to-morrow, and what is
true for me to-day may not yet be true for you. But a
table, you say, is always a table. Far from it, for to-day it
may be broken up and built into a fence, and in a
thousand years be petrified by water into stone or rotted
into mould. Only the laws of the Universe endure, and the
Life whose evolution they guide and help to express.

It may be argued that the foregoing principles hardly
constitute an object of meditation. The answer is that
once they are understood they may be applied to any
object, the more personal the better. You are smoking a
pipe. What are you doing? Inhaling the fumes from burning dead leaves. You object to that description, on the

MEDITATION ON THINGS AS THEY ARE

ground that smoking is a harmless habit? That is another question entirely; the fact remains that you are inhaling the fumes from burning dead leaves. If you wish to do so, do so by all means, but know what you are doing, even though the truth makes it seem less enjoyable. We live so much in a fool's paradise that it is well to wake up wherever and whenever possible. Cultivate a habit of ruthless realism, unceasingly asking and answering the question, 'What?' of all phenomena. At a later stage we will consider the question 'Why?'

Some find in this exercise a valuable aid to the control of sexual desire. Just as it is the imagination which feeds the flames in adolescence, so may the same imagination be used to control the fire. Analyze to yourself in frank and fullest detail the nature of the process involved, comparing it with animal mating, and meditating upon the disease and suffering which fills the world through its uncontrolled expression. Then, when anatomical, biological and the less pleasant aspects of the subject have been frankly and fully faced, consider the gaudy trappings of romance which the ingenuity and dishonest reasoning of lustful minds have added to the purely biological process of physical reproduction. If the desire still remains, as remain it will, for desire is not slain by reasoning, decide whether or not you will gratify it, but make your decision in the light of stark reality, and it may well be that with the imaginative faculty invoked as an aid and not a hindrance, desire, which is a handmaid of imagination, will come to heel.

Let it not be thought that this facing of facts, to the extent that our most imperfect senses can grasp the facts, is incompatible with the cult of beauty. The sound which a musician produces from a violin is none the less beautiful because produced by scraping horses' hair on cats' intestines. The beauty lies in the listener's mind, and is aroused by the rhythm, tone and pattern of sound evoked by the artist from his instrument. The beauty of the music is thus unaffected by the nature of the instrument from which it is produced. In the same way the human body is none the less beautiful because composed of humble elements. The elements are neither beautiful nor ugly, these qualities being the reactions of the beholder's mind. Learn, then, to form your own reaction to the beauty expressed by outward things, and refuse to be hide-bound by conventional ideas. Coal, for example, is by any standard a beautiful material, yet we do not find a gracefully shaped piece reposing with other lovely things in the drawing room cabinet.

This meditation on things as they are may be extended indefinitely, for Buddhism is based on a fearless and dispassionate examination of life's phenomena. From personal examples move on to analyze the ingredients of the daily round, and thence to current events of world importance. Then begin to consider causes, and so note how man is prone to limit his efforts at improvement to palliating effects. War, for example, is the outcome of hatred, which in turn is born of jealousy, greed and fear. Having traced back causes in national as well as personal acts, learn to view the future as the field of effects of causes being planted now, and so become wise on a larger scale of time. By this raising of consciousness above personal considerations on to the plane of causes one may watch

the ebb and flow of national and international movements and the cycles of natural and human evolution
and so, by an ever increasing ability to understand the
nature of things as they are, draw so much nearer to
Enlightenment.

3. *The Meditation on Dispassion*

This exercise follows naturally from the later stages of
the one before. It consists in achieving a focus of values
more truthful than our usual narrow point of view. Begin
by viewing the room in which you sit and those within it;
then in imagination view the whole house, the town in
which it is situated, and then extend your view until you
can visualize the nation as a whole. Already you will
observe that compared with the affairs of so many million
persons your own are of negligible importance, and if the
experiment be taken further, you will arrive in time at a
point of view when the earth itself may be viewed
objectively. Once more consider your own affairs in their
relation to the world, then add the whole solar system to
your mental vision, and plunge yet further into space until
the brain can hold no more. Now, with the immeasurable
majesty of the Universe around you, return in thought to
the confines of your room. Can you now be fretful over
some trivial personal circumstance? Will you not rather
laugh, and with this laughter show your sense of
humour, which is nothing more than a happy sense of
proportion, and a realization of the absurdity of utterly
disproportionate things?

Let the sweep of time be added to the immensity of
space. Think of a man of a hundred years of age, of a

castle a thousand years old, of a rock formation which it may have taken the sea a million years to fashion, of the time which must have passed since the light by which we now see the farthest star set out from that star to reach our eyes. How shall we view the impatience we were feeling, say, at the time it takes to learn to meditate? How, with this paralysing immensity of time and space before our mental eyes, can the element of self be allowed to dominate the field of view? Yet let this not be made an excuse for neglecting the little duties close at hand. We must learn to see the long view and the short view simultaneously, to think in terms of magnitude without losing sight of the humble yet no less important work which is waiting to be done. It has been said, 'There is nothing infinite apart from finite things.'

From such a detached and impersonal point of view one may begin to understand the Buddhist Chain of Causation as a complex inter-relation of cause-effect. In the previous exercise we began to examine the causes of particular results. By rising to the universal viewpoint above described one may the more easily understand the idea of simultaneous-dependent origination so picturesquely symbolized in the Buddhist Wheel of Life, for the doctrine applies, 'As above, so below,' and the laws of manifestation may be applied alike to man or the Universe.

Finally, as a corrective to too much concentration on the separative quality in dispassion, end this meditation with an exercise in pouring forth compassion for all forms of life, and strive to feel yourself as part of an indivisible unity.

4. *The Meditation on Motive*

Having answered to some extent the question 'What?', begin to cultivate an equally unceasing 'Why?', remembering that whereas it is well to assume the worst about one's own motives, for they are seldom as pure as they seem, it is wiser and more kind to assume the best in other people until the contrary be proved. This meditation naturally ranges over a far wider field than the springs of human action, but for most of us the important 'why?' to answer is that of motive.

Begin by examining your motives in little things. You decide to go the cinema. Why? To 'rest' your mind after a long day's work, as you explain to yourself, or to avoid the effort entailed by the serious study which the better side of you wishes to pursue? Or is it because your wife or a friend wants you to accompany them, and you lack the courage to refuse, or is it just that you feel a desire for the emotional 'kick' which you get from the modern sex-ridden films? Again, why do you get up when you do, and not earlier or later; why do you eat four meals a day instead of two, when you know quite well that two are enough for you; why do you buy new clothes when you do, and read the books you read? There are reasons; find out what they really are. You may be shocked at them. You will certainly be surprised.

Now analyze the motives for your opinions. As Miss Coster demands in her *Yoga and Western Psychology*, "How much of your opinion is based on family tradition, on fear of or desire for change, on class-prejudice, on fear of personal loss, on fear of seeming to be a crank? If your opinions were entirely based on emotion, on personal like and dislike, your problem would be far easier. It is the intricate confusion of fact and emotion, it is the skill with which personal desire presents to you perfectly adequate reasons for your cherished opinion that make the conflict so acute, and real candour so rare and so difficult."

Turn, now, to wider purposes. What, for example, is the purpose of the daily round itself? We are born, we grow, we are educated, we earn a living, marry, rear children, grow old, retire and die. What for? The question is one which increasing multitudes are asking, and students of the inner life must be prepared to answer it fully and carefully by an exposition of the Path, its purpose, nature and goal.

Finally, ask and answer the question honestly, 'Why do I meditate?' and if the answer be unsatisfactory, ask it again from time to time until it be as definite and one-pointed as the mind that meditates.

A useful extension of this exercise is an enquiry into the motives for doctrinal belief. Why do you believe in *karma* and rebirth? Is it because you have been brought up so to believe, or that your friends have persuaded you into such belief against your will, or because you would like these doctrines to be true and hope they are? Remember that there is no such thing as 'authority' for truth, and no doctrine is true for you until you have yourself examined it, tested it, and in the light of the intuition and experience found it to be true.

5. *Meditations on Particular Doctrines*

Consider for a moment the conception of Absolute

Truth. Such Truth is clearly unknowable as such by finite minds, yet it may be approached by symbol and analogy, and examined in the light of innumerable doctrines or laws, each of which is an aspect or facet of the whole. It follows that no one doctrine is Absolute-ly true, and it also follows that no doctrine can be immediately grasped in its entirety. There must be grades of understanding, and as we return again and again to the study of certain fundamental principles we attain an ever deeper realization of their meaning and their relation to one another. This in turn gives rise to an ever-increasing tolerance of different methods of approaching Truth, and of temporarily different points of view.

There is a general tendency to assume that because a doctrine is formulated in a manner easily assimilated by the intellect it may be understood. Yet between such intellectual assimilation and true understanding lies an interval of genuine hard work. Each doctrine or law must be taken as a subject for meditation and there analyzed, examined, compared with others, and then, as it were, assimilated by the intuition and thus for the first time understood. Only then will it become a mainspring of action and a force for spiritual development. One cannot apply a law or doctrine in one's daily life so long as it is but an idly held belief; only the dual process of deep meditation and experimental application will turn it from belief into a quality of character. For every man, for example, for whom the law of *karma* is a law of life as real as gravity there are ten for whom it is merely an unproductive theory. Yet it has been said that we only truly believe a doctrine when we behave as if it were true. Until

103

this moment arrives it is but mental food awaiting digestion, and as such of no value to the body corporate.

Make, then, a list of these laws and doctrines which you imagine you believe, and take them one by one. You may begin with those which are mentioned in the list of forty subjects for meditation set out in the Pali Canon, such as the Buddha, the Dhamma, the Sangha. What is meant by these? It may be that you have never asked yourself that question before. Consider, then, the three Signs of Being. Are there no more than three? Are these really true, or only half true? What is the relation between them? Do they spring from one another, and if so, which is cause and which effect? Pass on to the Four Noble Truths. Is the last Truth, the Noble Eightfold Path, Raja Yoga in another form, and wherein in it is there room for mysticism? What of the twin doctrines of *karma* and rebirth? Do they necessarily go together, and if so, what is reborn? Does *karma* apply to animals, the Arhat, the Gods? What are the Three Fires which bind men on the twelve spokes of the Wheel of Becoming, and how is one to escape from this Wheel? These are but a fraction of the countless questions one can put oneself to ensure that one possesses the necessary critical attitude to everything which claims to settle down in the mind as a belief. With the advent of cheap and simple literature on Buddhism there is so little effort needed to become acquainted with its basic principles that it is all too easy to forget that knowledge is useless until intuitively understood and intelligently applied. Begin again, then, in your study of 'Buddhism,' or whatever other '-ism' you are using at the moment as an approach to Truth, and having examined the doctrines of the Theravada, pass to those of the Mahayana, deciding, it may be for the first time, if the latter grew from the former, and how the two philosophies form together as complete a presentation of Truth as our minds are at present able to conceive. Finally, end your meditation with an effort to understand more deeply day by day that very basis of the Dhamma, the unity of life. Have you yet considered what this *does* imply, or is it still for you a charming but unpractical ideal?

Let those with imagination and the will to explore new fields of thought pass on to consider the relation between these various doctrines. What, for example, is the relation between *karma* and compassion? In *The Voice of the Silence* we read, "Compassion is no attribute. It is the law of laws, eternal harmony." Elsewhere we read that the key which opens one of the portals on the Way is *Shila*, described as "the key of Harmony in word and act, the key that counterbalances the cause and the effect, and leaves no further room for karmic action." Is there not a most illuminating truth concealed in this hint of relationship between compassion, *karma* and harmony?

After a while the doctrines thus examined by the intuition will cease to be so many static formulæ, and reveal themselves as dynamic forces which may be applied to self-regeneration in the same way that the laws of mechanics are used to materialize our vast conceptions of stone and steel.

6. *Meditation on the Self*

In a way, the Delphic exhortation, 'Know thyself,' is a summary of the whole purpose of meditation, for he who truly knows himself is master of the Universe. From this point of view this meditation includes all others. It will be found, however, that spiritual evolution ascends in spirals, and the student will find himself from time to time at a previous point in his ascent, but at a higher level. There is no ending to a study of the self, but the fact that no final understanding can be reached at the present stage of meditation is no reason for not beginning the study of a subject whose final secret will only be discovered at the threshold of Nirvana.

In a way this meditation is an extension of that on "Things as they are," for most of us are self-blinded to ourselves, and even to the fact that the self we know is an illusion, a changing and imperfect collection of attributes. Conceit, which is the child of desire and self-deceit, builds up an illusory self, a self-inflated balloon of egotism which must be destroyed at the first opportunity, for only when the bubble has been pricked, and the self, however humiliated, seen for what it is, can the foundation be laid for that self-reliance which is the crown of Buddhism. It is better to build on a small basis of solid rock than upon a superstructure of hollow and unsound material. Wherefore be wise, and be as ruthless in your self-analysis as your most unkindly friend.

There are two ways of meditating on the self, and sooner or later the student must genuinely appreciate that they are complementary. One way is to destroy the Not-Self, and the other is to cultivate the Self. The former is largely comprised under the heading of Character-building, and is the method used by the *Theravada* or Southern Buddhism. Its cry is an echo of the Brahmin "*Neti, neti*," meaning, "Not so, not so, this is not the Self." This is the doctrine of *anatta*, or not-*atta*, *atta* (*atman*) being the Brahmin word for Self.

The other, complementary, way is common to many schools of thought, both Eastern and Western, and is the way of all mystics. It consists of focussing the attention on the Ideal to the relative exclusion of all else, and proceeds by a progressive raising of consciousness through ever more spiritual levels until the individual is merged in the Ideal.

This method finds its supreme expression in the sixth chapter of the *Bhagavad Gita*, wherein of him who follows this way it is said: "When he hath abandoned every desire that ariseth from the imagination, and subdued with the mind the senses and organs which impel to action in every direction, being possessed of patience he by degrees finds rest; and having fixed his mind at rest in the true Self he should think of nothing else. To whatever object the inconstant mind goeth out he should subdue it, bring it back, and place it upon the Spirit. Supreme bliss surely cometh to the sage whose mind is thus at peace, whose passions and desires are thus subdued, who is thus in the true Self and free from sin." (Trans. W. Q. Judge.)

Each method has its advantages and disadvantages. Concentration on the illusory nature of the Not-Self has the advantage in the West of directly attacking our greatest weakness, the separative tendency of Western thought, which is the cause of our intensive egotism. On the other hand, a process which seems to imply complete disintegration of one's individuality has little appeal for those who, while vaguely realizing that the lower self has no eternal validity, yet refuse to believe that at its death there is nothing left behind. If this were so, they point out to those extremists who take the *anatta* doctrine literally, what is it that becomes purged of illusion, that 'having gained its freedom, knows that it is free,' that merges, ultimately, in Nirvana?

The complementary view, that all is Self, and that spiritual progress, is a moving towards reunion with the Ideal, has the merit of providing a tremendous spur to the raising of consciousness, but it is apt to blind the student to the very limitations of character which hold him back from his Ideal. Logically, the two methods are interchangeable, for it is, or should be, a matter of mere temperament whether one says of each of one's attributes or vehicles, "This is not I," until the Self has been disentangled from the last of them, or "The Self is the All and I am the Self," and steadily transforms the Ideal into actuality.

There are those who, to preserve the middle way, use either method alternatively, while others change their point of view on reaching the middle point of the ladder of consciousness. The meditation on the bodies, for example, is excellent for dissociating consciousness from its lower vehicles, but it is in a way moving backwards up the ladder, with one's back towards Reality. Let those to whom this point of view commends itself attempt this turning about. Having reached the point at which you can say with some conviction, "I am not my body, my emotions, or my thought-machine," you will find yourself in a world of abstract thought, of creative ideation as illuminated by the intuition. Here are still limitations of form, though infinitely more tenuous, but even here is not the Self, which lies behind you still. Then turn your back on the lower self and face that Life whose body is the Universe, that Absolute Reality of which no words can tell. Let fall the veils which blind you from your inheritance, for as they fall so will your consciousness expand until it is commensurate with the Universal Consciousness. Here only is the Self, that no man has the right to call his own, and yet the Self of which each unit of existence is an aspect not yet merged into the whole.

One would think that these methods were clearly complementary, yet there are those who still imagine that the Buddha taught that because there is no abiding Self in the five *skandhas*, or constituents of personality, there is therefore no Self to use those vehicles. But the Signs of Being, imperfection, variability and *anatta*, or Not-Self, apply to *Samsara*, the world of manifestation, whereas the opposite pole of being, *Nirvana*, would exhibit, were it not beyond all attributes, those of perfection, changelessness and Self. Let those who cling to this nihilistic and depressing doctrine turn to the *Dhammapada's* opening words, that the key to all phenomena is the mind. Here is the fulcrum about which our complex being turns. When the mind is immersed in matter it cannot see the light, but when raised to higher levels it tends to move towards its own place, which is the state of perfection called Nirvana, a "blowing out" or extinguishing of all those elements of being which separate the part from the whole. The higher aspect of the mind may be called for the sake of convenience the soul, so long as it be clearly understood that it is not in any sense immortal, while the lower, the concrete mind or thought machine, though a necessary vehicle of consciousness, is called 'the great slayer of the Real,' for it harbours the great 'heresy of separateness,' the illusion that any unit of life can legitimately have interests and aims antagonistic to the commonweal. Only when the lower is purged of illusion and merged into the higher is the latter free to leave Samsara, and so, by merging into Life itself, find immortality.

7. *The Meditation on Analogy*

Analogy is one of the most valuable aids to an understanding of the inner life. 'As above, so below'. Man is the microcosm of the Universe. It is not only in the solemn wonder of the sunset or the flight of birds that wisdom speaks to us. The lower mind which dominates the West to-day may find its symbols in mechanical and homely things. Consider, as one example, the moving stairways in the Tube. Here is a simple analogy of the cycle of life and death, the alternation of extremes we call the pairs of opposites. Each stairway visibly moves up or down, yet all invisibly the opposite movement is taking place at precisely the same speed. Here in miniature is a 'wheel of becoming,' bearing its burden of lives unceasingly, while the pair of stairways, ever ascending and descending, present a mechanical model of the whole field of cosmogenesis.

Again, the gears of a car provide analogies for the regulation and technique of work and rest, and to watch a bargee on the river using the force of the tides to do his bidding is a lesson in how best to handle the rhythms of events. Consider again the orderly disorder of a modern factory, the patterned flow of countless apparently disconnected processes moving to an organized and definite end. The cinema is full of useful analogy to those with inner eyes, and do we realize, we who know the unlimited power of the human mind, that our thoughts are 'broadcasting' at an individual wave-length each hour of the day? In the flowers in the window box we may watch rebirth; in our own and our neighbours' lives the impersonal hand of *karma* teaching lessons which are patiently repeated until learnt. In brief, we must learn to moralize, not with the unctuous insincerity of Victorian times, but as students in Life's university. In this way one may extract a spiritual lesson from the humblest incident and thus, as Shakespeare puts is, "Find tongues in trees, books in the running brooks, sermons in stones and good in everything."

The Four Brahma Viharas

The four *Brahma Viharas*, variously translated as Sublime Moods or Divine States (of mind) have come to occupy such a central position in the field of Buddhism that they cannot be omitted from a list of subjects for meditation, especially as they are included in the forty subjects mentioned in the Pali Canon.

The four meditations are examined and compared in the ninth chapter of the *Visuddhi Magga* of Buddhaghosha, but the following quotation from the *Maha-Sudassana Sutta* summarizes the nature and purpose of the exercise. "And he lets his mind pervade one-quarter of the world with thoughts of Love, with thoughts of Compassion, with thoughts of sympathetic Joy and with thoughts of Equanimity; and so the second quarter, and so the third, and so the fourth. And thus the whole wide world, above, below, around and everywhere does he continue to pervade with heart of Love, Compassion, Joy and Equanimity, far-reaching, great, beyond measure, free from the least trace of anger or ill-will." In the Love meditation the meditator radiates his thought-force as it were horizontally; Compassion looks downward towards the world of suffering, just as Joy looks upward to the world of happiness, leaving Equanimity to restore the balance disturbed by self-identification with these two extremes.

Love

Buddhism has been described as a cold religion, but it is easy to collate passages from the Pali Canon which shows the high place that *Metta*, loving-kindness, held in the Buddha's teaching, and this in spite of the fact that Buddhism is essentially a way of enlightenment and not of emotional mysticism. Moreover, loving-kindness as practised by the Buddhist is a deliberate and sustained attitude of mind, as distinct from a spontaneous exhibition of feeling. Love that springs from centres lower than the creative mind is all too easily replaced by hate, or at least capable of so narrow a focus that hatred of some other person may exist in the mind at the same moment. Not so with the Buddhist who practises the first of the four *Brahma Viharas*. He first suffuses his own being with unbounded love, partly, as the cynical commentator puts it, because oneself is the easiest of all persons to love, and partly because love must first be built in as a quality of the meditator's mind before he can habitually broadcast it to the world. Having suffused himself with the quality of love he turns in thought to a friend, and finds it easy to suffuse his friend with the same quality. It is suggested by the commentator that for various reasons it is best that the friend chosen should be of the same sex and still living. The meditator then turns to a more difficult task, the suffusing of some person towards whom he feels indifferent, neither affectionate nor hostile, yet the same quality and quantity of affection must now be sent to him as was more gladly sent to the friend. Next, and most difficult, he visualizes an enemy, should there still be a fellow being for whom he feels antipathy, and even though at first it is difficult to do so without a feeling of hypocrisy, suffuses him with the warmth of generous and pure affection. In so doing he has no ulterior motive in his mind, though the effect of his action will be to slay the enmity. Finally, he radiates his loving-kindness to all mankind, then to all forms of life, and so through all the Universe until with an intensive effort of the will which carries him far into the *Jhanas*, or higher states of consciousness, he becomes as it were the very spirit of love, and on return to normal consciousness continues to radiate this power to all around him. He thus, from the plane of thought, joins hands with the Bhakti Yogi and the Western religious mystic, many of whom achieve the same result through purified emotion and desire.

Compassion

To the extent that *Karuna*, compassion, is an emotion

at all, it is the Buddhist emotion *par excellence*. Not without reason is the Buddha called the All-Compassionate One as well as the All-Enlightened One. Yet Compassion is no mere attribute of mind. At its higher levels it includes both love and joy, and even equanimity, for it consists in an understanding love, a blend of emotion-intellect illumined by the intuition. Wherefore is it said in *The Voice of Silence*, "Compassion is no attribute. It is the LAW of Laws—eternal Harmony, a shoreless universal essence, the light of everlasting Right and fitness of all things, the law of love eternal." Again, in a footnote it is described as "an abstract, impersonal law whose nature, being absolute Harmony, is thrown into confusion by discord, suffering and sin."

Buddhism has been fairly described as the religion of suffering, for it realizes as none other that suffering is a quality inherent in all forms of life, however blinded those immersed in the illusion of pleasure may be to the limitations inherent in the world of becoming. It is true that suffering is too strong a term to use as the sole equivalent of the Pali *dukkha*, for the term is, of course, only relative, and covers conditions ranging from the most acute physical and mental agony to a purely metaphysical understanding of the state of incompleteness or imperfection which is a necessary corollary to the law of *anicca*, the law of change. But every form of life is subject to the sway of *dukkha*, and the meditator who is radiating compassion is advised by the commentator to begin with persons in the depths of misery, towards whom the springs of compassion flow easily, and then to enlarge the ambit of his thought to include ever more varied and subtle forms

114

of disharmony, maladjustment and dis-ease, mental and emotional as well as physical, until once more his range is commensurate with the Universe. In such a way he will draw just so much nearer the incomparable ideal set forth in *The Voice of the Silence*: "Let thy Soul lend its ear to every cry of pain like as the lotus bares its heart to drink the morning sun. Let not the fierce Sun dry one tear of pain before thyself hast wiped it from the sufferer's eye. But let each burning human tear drop on thy heart and there remain; nor ever brush it off until the pain that caused it is removed."

Joy

The value of this exercise lies in the effect it has on envy and jealousy, modes of thought which definitely cramp the thinker's mind. The mind which responds whole-heartedly at news of a friend's success or happiness, even though it be attained at the expense of its own, is free from the destructive jealousy which, rooted in egotism, is too often the father of hate. The essence of the exercise lies in being glad on another's account, and is thus an excellent antidote to the narrow claims of self; hence the translation of *mudita* as "sympathetic joy." Here again, begin the exercise by thinking of a friend who is filled with joy at some good fortune, whether physical or mental, and then enlarge the scope of thought to cover all who rejoice for any reason, whether the cause for rejoicing be in your eyes sufficient or no.

Equanimity

It is difficult to find an English word to represent *upekkha*. Detachment is sometimes used, as also dispassion

115

and serenity. The idea is conveyed in the stanza of the *Sutta Nipata*. "A heart untouched by worldly things, a heart that is not swayed by sorrow, a heart passionless, secure, that is the greatest blessing." The same idea is echoed in Kipling's immortal lines "If you can meet with Triumph and Disaster, and treat those two imposters just the same." Its essence lies in rising above the self-identification with others' feelings which is to some extent involved in the radiations of compassion and joy. As the commentator says, "The salient characteristic of equanimity is evolving a central position towards others, its function is seeing others impartially, its manifestation is the quenching of both aversion and sycophancy, its proximate cause is the seeing how each belongs to the continuity of his own karma." It must not, however, be confused with indifference, which is the outcome of a closing of the mind to others' suffering and joy, and therefore the very opposite of the virtue of compassion. It is in the words of the *Bhagavad Gita*, "A constant unwavering steadiness of heart upon the arrival of every event whether favourable or unfavourable," and is achieved by moving in consciousness towards a central point of view, so that events are viewed from the source of causes instead of the circumference of the circle where they show forth as effects. Strive to infuse your own mind with this quality, then feel it equally towards a friend and enemy, and so by gradual stages to all forms of life, thus, after passing through love, compassion and sympathetic joy, returning to that inner equilibrium which the outward events of daily life should be unable to destroy.

CHAPTER SIX

Character Building

THERE ARE as many methods of meditation as there are meditators, but the final goal is always the same. The immediate goal, however, is generally concerned with the moulding of character or with the raising of consciousness, the relationship between the two being well expressed in Talbot Mundy's *Om* (p. 16): "He who would understand the Plains must ascend the Eternal Hills, where a man's eyes scan Infinity. But he who would make use of understanding must descend on to the Plains, where Past and Future meet and men have need of him."

The importance of character building lies in the need of a sound foundation for the mighty structure of an enlightened mind. For thought is force, and it is useless to acquire tremendous power if it is to be used for evil ends, and thus accomplish nought but self-destruction. The recent war presented an unforgettable picture of the misuse of science by nations whose knowledge had outrun morality, but if it is easy to misuse such forces of nature as are now at the command of science, it is far easier to misuse the powers of mind developed in meditation. Hence the danger of looking upon meditation as an end in itself, or worse, as an end which will give but personal power, instead of regarding it as only one means of helping all humanity along the path of self-forgetfulness. Yet if the powers developed in lower meditation are considerable, the forces evolved in higher meditation are more powerful still. Hence the importance of paying increasing attention to character building in order to keep pace with the increasing powers developed by the mind.

The subject is vast, and it is impossible here to do more than suggest certain guiding principles for achieving maximum results with the minimum of wasted effort. In the first place, it is well to appreciate that the task is more laborious than inherently difficult. No man with the necessary determination and patience can fail to achieve, comparatively quickly, an improvement in character. Success is the reward of quiet, unremitting effort rather than of intermittent bursts of energy, and it is a type of work which may be, and ultimately must be, practised at all times of the day. The student is therefore advised to regard the methodical improvement of character as the true day's work, and the world of wage-earning and social activities as a school wherein to learn those principles of action which must sooner or later be built in as qualities. This is no exercise for leisure hours alone, nor is there any man or woman who may not practise it all the time. Time and space limit the body but need not limit the mind. An invalid in bed for life, the prisoner behind unyielding bars, the man who claims that he would do so much had he the time and opportunity, all can learn to use the mind constructively for the deliberate elimination of unwanted habits of thought and action, and their replacement by those virtues whose absence or distortion we label vice.

Above all, cultivate strength of mind. Better a strong mind wasting its energy in unproductive channels than a mind too weak to move at all, for the former will sooner or later learn its error and change direction, but the mind which does not move at all has not yet become a follower of the All-Enlightened One. One is reminded of the story of an utterly ineffective individual who approached a Master and enquired, from a heart that yearned to be of service, "Master, what may I do to help humanity?" And the Master, with eyes of understanding, looked down upon the questioner and said: "What *can* you do?" It must not be forgotten that there is an age-old maxim to the effect that "Nature spews the lukewarm from her mouth." To the same effect is a verse in the *Dhammapada*: "That which ought to be done, do with all vigour. A half-hearted follower of the Buddha spreads much evil around." It is not merely that strength of mind is needed both for destroying evil and acquiring good, but that a negative inaction may of itself be evil. As is said in *The Voice of the Silence*, "Inaction in a deed of mercy becomes an action in a deadly sin."

Generally speaking, it is better to begin the task of self-improvement in the mind, leaving outward habits to be altered in due course as the inevitable outcome of new modes of thought. Concentrate on essentials, and remember that food and dress, for example, are not essentials, and of little importance in the reckoning of spiritual worth.

Yet waste no time in pausing to measure your inward growth. We have no standards for spiritual improvement, and such a habit leads to the very egotism which character building tries to destroy. Likewise avoid comparisons. You have no means of telling whether your neighbour is more or less 'advanced' than yourself, and it is vanity alone which prompts the enquiry. It is enough to know that

119

there are always forms of life above us and forms of life below. Finally, cultivate a sense of humour, for the man who can laugh at himself, and even at his own efforts in self-improvement, is safe from the labyrinth of self-delusion in which so many students spend such wearisome and unproductive days.

Dana

The systems of moral development are countless but there is great wisdom in that which lies at the heart of Buddhism. *Dana*, charity, *Sila*, the moral life, and *Bhavana*, mind-development, is the summary of human progress set out in the Pali Scriptures, and it is interesting to note the order in which the factors in the triple process are given. Before *Sila* is even begun, attention must be paid to *Dana*, for until the student has made of his mind a conduit pipe of spiritual force, eagerly handing on to all in need of it the fruits of his own experience, he will, like a vessel with no outlet, be unable, being filled, to hold any more. Hence the law proclaimed in *The Voice of the Silence*, "Point out the 'Way'—however dimly, and lost among the host—as does the evening star to those who tread their path in darkness," and hence the important statement on the preceding page of the same manual. "To live to benefit mankind is the first step. To practise the six glorious virtues is the second." This mental attitude is the true meaning of charity, for until the heart of compassion is awakened an outward gift has little value to the giver, and may even be the cause of harm to the recipient. Cultivate, then, what W. Q. Judge described as "the mental devotion which strains to give," and so experience in time what the Taoists call the "emptying of the heart," which alone leads to that spiritual poverty enjoined by every Teacher of the Way. Only when one has achieved a little of such experience do the exhortations of great Teachers on this subject cease to be platitudes. "Give up thy life if thou wouldst live" is a statement of fact as definite as "Foregoing self, the Universe grows 'I'," but one must begin by giving up, in the sense of loosening one's attachment to little things, before learning the very meaning of the 'Great Renunciation.' But once this principle is fairly established in the mind one's attitude towards outward charity is radically changed. Instead of carelessly giving away a certain percentage of one's worldly goods one should learn to regard *all* one's property as already given to mankind, and henceforth merely held in trust for their benefit. Money, for example, is a form of power, and therefore calls for wise and thoughtful handling, and he who has more than he needs is fortunate in the possession of tremendous opportunity for doing good. Yet the responsibility is equally tremendous, and of all who think, "If only I could afford to help with money in this or that direction . . ." there are few indeed who would be able, were their dreams to be suddenly materialised, to use the power of money wisely and well.

Yet all may make a small beginning, not only by thoughtfully applying to others' needs the surplus which remains from their own necessity, but by working to increase that surplus with this end in view. As is said in a Mahayana scripture, "Therefore should we encourage small desire that we may have to give to him who needs."

Sila

Sila covers the subject under review, just as *Bhavana* includes concentration and meditation. It is the field in which to apply Right Effort, that is, "To prevent new evil entering one's mind; to remove all evil that is there; to develop such good as is in one's mind; to acquire still more unceasingly." One can plan out a system of moral development by striving to obey the five Buddhist 'precepts' against killing, stealing, sexual excess, slander and intoxication, at the same time building in the positive, complementary virtues, or one can summarise the work to be done as the extinguishing or allowing to die out of the 'Three Fires' of *Dosa*, hatred, *Lobha*, lust, and *Moha*, illusion. In either case remember that these virtues are moral principles and not mere physical habits, and that each term covers a far wider range of mental activity than is conventionally implied. The New Testament reminder, for example, that he who lusteth after a woman in his heart has already committed adultery with her, is an example of the way in which the spirit and not the letter of a moral law must be obeyed.

Asceticism

But whatever the system chosen let it follow the Middle Way. Avoid extremes, even of self-denial, and if for the sake of gaining a greater self-control you impose upon yourself a series of self-denying practices, remember that their only value lies in the extent to which they enable the will to control its vehicles. The nature of the exercises is of no importance, though it is well to begin with those which do not arouse too fierce an opposition in order to acquire the strength to achieve more difficult results. For example, to give up breakfast for a week will do you no harm, though you will find your mind at once invaded with a host of excellent reasons why you should abandon such an uncomfortable decision. More difficult, because more subtle, are practices which attack an ingrained habit of thought. Try, for example, refraining from using the word 'I' for a single hour of ordinary conversation, and you will understand the meaning of the word egotism. Nor are the senses easy to control, even when there is no moral implication in what you are for-bidding them to do. Try walking down a line of shops without once glancing in any of them, or refrain for a whole train journey from once glancing at the face of the person opposite. From such elementary exercises, turn to muscle control. How long can *you* stand with one arm held straight above the head? Yet there are countless men in India who do so until the arm withers. This is, of course, the very extreme which the Buddha condemned as unprofitable, but one cannot help admiring the tremen-dous strength of will which can enforce such muscular obedience.

Desire

All this effort at self-control, however, would be un-necessary could one learn to control the desires of the personality, for if these desires were brought into harmony with the ideals of the higher mind there would be no need of the will to enforce obedience. Hence the Buddha's injunction, quoted in the *Dhammapada*: "Not through discipline and vows, nor depth of learning, nor by attainments in meditation nor by living apart do I earn the bliss no worlding ever knows. O, bhikkhus, be not confident until ye reach the destruction of desire." Every student will notice that these desires are strongest in youth, and that age of itself produces a certain desirelessness. Yet there is no merit in controlling a desire which has died. It is while the self is fired with youthful vigour that its desires must be in all their strength controlled and directed into higher purposes, for only then can the full strength of one's faculties be freed from the tyranny of outward things, and set "to storm the ramparts of Reality". Be on the watch, therefore, for the glib tongue of desire, for his is the voice which speaks through envy, meanness, lust, dishonesty and a host of other vices which die when desire is dead.

The Elimination of Vice

There remains the vexed question of the right attitude to vices, using the term to cover all those habits of mind we would fain eradicate. First, as to the nature of evil. We know that "all we are is the result of what we have thought; it is founded on our thoughts, it is made up of our thoughts," and evil is no exception. As is pointed out in the *Mahatma Letters to A. P. Sinnett*, "Evil has no existence *per se* and is but the absence of good and exists but for him who is made its victim. . . . The real evil proceeds from human intelligence and its origin rests entirely with reasoning man who dissociates himself from Nature. Humanity alone is the true source of evil. Evil is the exaggeration of good, the progeny of human selfishness." If this be not clear beyond all questioning, let the

124

student study the rest of the famous Letter 10 from which these brief quotations have been made. The sources of evil are given in a Buddhist Scripture as desire, hatred, delusion and fear. In other words, impelled by these qualities within his mind a man commits acts whose karmic consequences he finds he does not like and therefore labels evil. These causes, the producers of evil, are therefore labelled vices, and it follows that in order to remove the evil we must remove the vicious qualities.

The process of removal is two-fold, to dissociate oneself from the undesirable quality, or, to use the psychological term, to objectivise it, and then to use the most suitable of the three alternative methods available for its elimination. It has been said that all that we regard as independent of ourselves we can master, but over that which we believe to be ourselves we have no power. Before, therefore, we can begin to remove an unwanted quality we must, as it were, stand back and look at it. So long as a man identifies himself with hatred for example, he cannot control his hate. As has been pointed out, he might as well try to lift himself up by his belt. Regard yourself, therefore, as a scientist, and lay the offending vice upon the laboratory table. Examine it, analyse its cause, its nature and its results, and face the fact that you are allowing it to dominate your mind. Such an exercise, which is really psycho-analysis self-administered, will in the vast majority of cases prepare the way for one of the three principal methods of elimination, all of which have the merit that they do not increase the strength of the vice by thinking about it. For thought is power, and to think of a quality tends to strengthen it.

Each of the three methods, avoidance, replacement and sublimation, is best for certain faults and failings, and one must choose which ever is most suitable. One cannot, for example, very well sublimate anger, although love can easily replace it. Sexual thoughts, on the other hand, are best handled by the process of sublimation, while other temptations may be avoided altogether.

1. *By Avoidance*

There are those who struggle fiercely with their failings, and use much energy in the unceasing war. They have *The Voice of the Silence* as their authority. "Strangle thy sins, and make them dumb for ever, before thou dost lift one foot to mount the ladder." Yet though it is abundantly true that by one method or another all vice must be overcome, the choice of method is in the student's hands. The method of avoidance, is to give up thinking about the vice at all, and to keep the mind so filled with nobler thoughts that the undesirable quality, like a forgotten fire, dies out for lack of fuelling. You will naturally make this practice very much easier by carefully avoiding those things and persons and places which tend to stimulate your mind into the wrong way of thought. The man who tends to drink too much is best away from companions who drink too much, and the conceited man is best away from flatterers. Nor is there any shame in thus avoiding temptation. Why make the task of moral purification unnecessarily difficult? The basic principle of *Judo*, the Japanese science of wrestling which is based on Buddhist philosophy, has been described as victory by giving way, and the mind that can learn to avoid an evil thought has gained its end with far less effort than by fighting it. Yet do not fall into the trap of imagining that a vice can be overcome by letting it have its way. What is said of lust in *The Voice of the Silence* applies to every form of evil. "Do not believe that lust can ever be killed out if gratified or satiated, for this is an abomination inspired by Mara. It is by feeding vice that it expands and waxes strong, like to the worm that fattens on the blossom's heart."

2. *By Replacement*

Closely allied to the above method, although not quite the same, is the elimination of faults by substituting in the mind the opposite quality whenever the failing raises its unwanted head. Its essence is contained in the famous stanza from the *Dhammapada*: "Hatred ceases not by hatred, hatred ceases but by love." Supposing, for example, that one feels dislike for an individual. Try the effect of deliberately arousing in the mind a pure affection, and direct this force towards him, either at definite intervals or whenever his existence comes to mind. Only experiment will prove the amazing results of such an exercise. First, one's own antipathy will be steadily reduced until it vanishes, and secondly, the one-time enemy will gradually appear in a better light. By the power of love one will see virtues in him hitherto unnoticed, and thirdly, the same force will arouse its like in him. All who have genuinely tried this experiment agree that it is one of the most beautiful, because most purely spiritual uses of the power of thought possessed by every mind. Remember that the mind can only hold one of two opposite forces at a time, and if the right force be the usual inhabitant it will automatically repel its opposite. In time this process will become automatic.

In order to train the mind to achieve this valuable habit, it is useful to carry in one's pocket for use at spare moments one of the numerous booklets in which the spiritual wisdom of the world is now enshrined. The following are examples: *The Voice of the Silence,* the *Bhagavad Gita, The Light of Asia, Practical Occultism,* the *Tao Te Ching, The Sutra of Hiu Neng* and, last but not least, the *Dhammapada.* Another method is to commit to memory some of the short poems in which occult truths are to be found, such as Kipling's *If,* or some of the short speeches in Shakespeare's plays.

3. *By Sublimation*

A third method, which is the best for certain failings, is that of sublimation. There is a fine passage in Hartmann's *Magic* quoted in *Practical Occultism* which explains it well: "Accumulated energy cannot be annihilated; it must be transferred to other forms, or be transformed into other modes of motion; it cannot remain for ever inactive and yet continue to exist. It is useless to attempt to resist a passion which we cannot control. If its accumulating energy is not led into other channels, it will grow until it becomes stronger than will and stronger than reason. To control it, you must lead it into another and higher channel. Thus a love for something vulgar may be changed by turning it into a love for something high, and vice may be changed into virtue by changing its aim."

This method is the best for learning to control the

creative force which on the physical plane we call sex. The root of the 'sex problem' seems to be the failure to distinguish between control and suppression. Man can harness the fiercest mountain stream but he may not dam the humblest rivulet without providing an outlet for its energy. So with sex, a clean, impersonal creative force, as natural as water in a river bed, as restless and tremendous as the sea. On the physical plane we call it sex, on the emotional plane it functions as artistic temperament, enthusiasm and emotional power, while in the realm of mind it is that instinct to create, the 'creative urge' which is responsible for all that man has ever made, inclusive of himself. Herein lies the essence of sublimation, to choose the channel through which the force shall flow. It is but a gradual withdrawing of the creative force from purely physical to higher levels by the exercise of ceaseless vigilance and self-control.

In all these methods, and they are but aspects of one method, choose that which is most suited to the failing under consideration, and refuse to compromise in carrying it out. It is better to fail in attempting to do what you know to be right, and then to admit your failure frankly, than to succeed by way of a speciously argued compromise. At any and every stage of the ascent of the ladder of becoming there is always that which is at that stage definitely right and that which is definitely wrong. Then, follow the right unswervingly, at whatever cost to the personality, and whatever the ignorant may think or say. There is no shame in failure save in the failure to attempt and it is better to fail a thousand times in an attempt to achieve a clearly perceived ideal than to succeed in a poor,

dishonest compromise. As Tennyson wrote in his
Œnone, our ideal should be

"To live by law,
Acting the law we live by without fear;
And, because right is right, to follow right
Were wisdom in the scorn of consequence."

CHAPTER SEVEN

The Culture of the Emotions

SO FAR this manual has concerned itself with the culture of the mind, using the term as equivalent to the intellect or 'thought-machine,' but just as perfect physical development includes each function of the body, so mind development must include each function or aspect of the mind. Hence the inclusion at this point of a brief chapter on the emotions in which to consider their nature, use and dangers, and the importance of their culture and control.

The Nature of Emotion

In the space available it is not possible to survey the discoveries and rival theories of modern psychologists, but this much is generally accepted and may be verified by experience. The life-force, or *libido*, the energy which expresses itself through countless ever-changing forms, functions, so far as the personality is concerned, through thought and action, using the former term to include the complex processes of ideation and the latter to include such 'mental action' as the deliberate radiation of ideas. The perfect act is an idea completely manifest, and in the perfect union of thought and act there will be no force left over and unused. But most actions are far from perfect, and there remains a certain residuum of un-expanded force analogous to the steam produced in a railway engine which is not used in pulling the train. This residuum of force is called emotion, the amount produced depending on many factors, but always being proportionate to the mind's capacity, using the term to denote the strength of the engine or machine. But whether weak or strong, and whether large or small in proportion to the energy produced, this emotion must in one way or another be expressed or liberated. It may be expressed directly through the nervous system and appear in gesture, words, or even physical violence. It may, on the other hand, remain invisible to the eye of all save the trained psychologist. Thirdly, it may be diverted into phantasy, imaginative action, and fourthly, be either genuinely controlled or sublimated into higher forms.

But, it may be argued, emotion seems to be the product of sense-reaction. The sight of cruelty, for example, may arouse the emotion of anger, and the sound of an explosion may arouse the emotion of fear. But unless there is present in the mind from past experience a residuum of un-expanded force which such an outside stimulus can arouse, there will be no emotional response, though the same stimulus may give birth to rapid thought and appropriate action. It follows that the more perfectly developed and controlled the mind, the less force will be wasted in emotion.

These basic principles must be thoroughly mastered before the culture of the emotions can be usefully begun. Once so mastered they may be applied by the student to the functioning of emotion in his own, his neighbours' or in group psychology, but the space available forbids that these ramifications be further considered here. It will be found, however, that emotion, like every other aspect of the one life-force, is dual in manifestation, the lower aspect reflecting *kama*, sensuous desire, while the higher emotions reflect the faculty of spiritual knowledge, generally called the intuition. The foregoing principles, together with the methods of culture which follow, apply particularly to the lower emotions, for the higher are best considered as reflections of spiritual forces which rank far higher than the thought-machine.

This classification of the contents of one's complex being may be of value in the process of self-development, but it must not be forgotten that there is but one life-force, and that all the planes and sub-planes of our being are but vehicles of consciousness, which is the personal aspect of the Universal Life. It follows that the same aspect of this one life-force may manifest on different levels, just as a single aspect of cosmic force, for example, electricity, may appear in many forms. The higher emotions may therefore be regarded either as emotions or as qualities pertaining to a higher level of consciousness. Joy, for example, as distinct from ephemeral pleasure, has its source in spiritual experience, and pertains, to use a scientific analogy, to light rather than to heat. It may be regarded as a form of spiritual illumination, in which the mind for a fleeting moment glimpses the bliss of true enlightenment. The same applies to compassion and the higher forms of love. Hence the importance of practising the four *Brahma Viharas*, whether these be regarded as sublimated emotions or as mental qualities illumined by the intuition.

The Dangers of Emotion

From the foregoing it will be seen that emotion is a waste of energy in that it produces of itself no useful results. It is, however, more than a mere waste of power, for it deludes the mind into accepting it as intuition, wears out the physical body before its time, and clouds the light of reason.

Emotion is connected on the one hand with instinct and on the other with intuition, and it needs considerable experience to discriminate between the two. It is often said that women are more intuitive than men. They are certainly more emotional, and hence, it is said, more easily in touch with the intuition, but much that is claimed as the voice of the intuition is only the subtle voice of desire. The acid test for all such flashes of irrational belief is that laid down by the Buddha as the only true 'authority'. Does the knowledge thus acquired agree with previous experience, with knowledge already found to be true? If so, it may well be accepted as provisionally true; if not, it is well to beware before acting upon an impulse which runs contrary to reason and past experience. Herein lies the value of the more cumbrous approach to the intuition through the intellect, for a truth which stands upon the foundations of close reasoning must sooner or later be ratified by the light of intuition, whereas feeling unsupported by such reasoning *may* be true, but may, as already pointed out, be merely the voice of desire in another guise.

But even when feeling has not been raised to the level of intuitive perception it may supply the driving force or

enthusiasm for progress towards the ideal. In the words of
Evelyn Underhill in *The Life of the Spirit and the Life of
To-day*, "The function of feeling is to increase the energy
of the idea. The cool, judicious type of belief will never
possess the life-changing power of a more fervid, though
perhaps less rational faith." This is true, if full attention
be given to the word belief. It is only when belief is
merged into conviction that will is harnessed to the idea,
and thought harmoniously expressed in action. In the
perfectly developed mind thought and feeling are so
wedded to action that from their union there is nothing
left behind. Enthusiasm is in this sense a quality of
mind, and to the extent that it manifests as emotion is a
waste of power.

But emotion has more positive dangers, for it unduly
exhausts the body and clouds the mind. Hence the definite
pronouncement of the Master K.H. to his pupil A. P.
Sinnett in words which seem at first to militate against
compassion, but which in fact bear out the magnificent
description of true compassion as "the Law of Laws,
eternal harmony". "The passions, the affections, are not to
be indulged in by him who seeks to KNOW, for they
'wear out the earthly body with their own secret power,
and he who would gain his aim *must be cold*'. He must not
even desire too earnestly or too passionately the object he
would reach; else the very wish will prevent the possibility
of its fulfilment, at best, retard it and throw it back." Here
is a point at which many an attack has been launched at
Buddhism, that it is so "cold". In the sense that it knows
the dangers of emotion the charge is true, but in what
religion or teaching is there to be found a nobler expres-

sion of true compassion than that which emanates from the heart of Buddhism? There is such a force as spiritual love and compassion which is far above the equivalent emotions, and functions rather through the higher aspects of the mind. The deliberate cultivation of such qualities renders their emotional equivalents unnecessary, and thus reduces to a minimum their power to cloud the mind. As Miss Tillyard says in *Spiritual Exercises*, "The state of mind recommended to the Buddhist is not one of religious enthusiasm. It is qne of grave benevolence to his fellow men, and of inner serenity and detachment. The aspirant is carefully warned not to disquiet himself with any emotion, however excellent. . . ." Emotion, by tending towards the personal, hinders the cool, dispassionate examination of laws and principles which leads to enlightenment. Pure thought is always impersonal, and emotion, which is linked with desire and therefore inevitably personal, introduces factors which obscure the issue and make cool judgement far more difficult.

But, it may be argued, both art and mysticism spring from the emotions. Is this common assumption true? Art is an expression of impersonal beauty through a personal medium, and it will be found that the greatest art, of whatever country and whatever time, is the most impersonal. Beauty is the outward appearance of cosmic harmony, and art is an attempt by human beings to interpret beauty in another form. It follows that the measure of artistic genius is the extent to which eternal values are exhibited before the senses, whether the medium used be poetry or pottery, music or the movements of the human form. In such portrayal of eternal qualities the intrusion of the personal is only permitted to the extent that the personal element is common to all mankind, and to this extent it is impersonal. Where, then, in such portrayal, is there room for emotion, either in the artists or in the beholder's mind? True, the artist must be super-sensitive, but the senses should be outposts of the mind, while the greatest art arouses in the beholder a faculty far higher than the emotions, that by which the mind attains direct perception of the laws of cosmic harmony which the artist has successfully portrayed.

As for the mystic, if it be argued that he seeks and finds enlightenment through emotion, the answer is threefold; first, that most of the great mystics have built the intensity of their devotion on the foundation of a noble intellect; secondly, that the guiding light of the true mystic is an intuition which is dimmed rather than made brighter by excessive feeling; and thirdly, that the emotion, if it can be so described, by which the greatest mystics have been most conspicuous is a profound serenity of mind, produced by a vision of true values and of life's immeasurable unity.

This serenity, enables the student to rise above the contending forces of attraction and repulsion, and to grow as indifferent to moral as to physical pain. The emotions, like the mind, must be trained to mirror the Ideal, and this is impossible while they respond under the impulse of desire to every whim and fancy of the personality. Only when they have been trained no longer to respond to outside stimulus will they cease to be a source of confusion to the mind, for emotion, as already pointed out, makes clarity of thought impossible.

The Culture of the Emotions

It may seem curious that one should speak of the culture of a force which is described as a useless by-product of thought. But it must never be forgotten that force is one, though manifesting in innumerable forms, and as all but the most advanced students are constantly generating emotion it is only right that such force should be utilized or sublimated into higher forms. As mind development proceeds through the higher ranges of meditation, less and less force will be wasted in emotion. Meanwhile, let such of the life-force as does so manifest be harnessed to spiritual purposes.

The culture of the emotions is analogous to that of the mind, and many of the same considerations apply. It will be noted, for example, that both thought and feeling react upon the physical vehicle. The West is slowly beginning to observe the effect of thought and emotion on physical health, and to note the way in which worry, for example, reacts through the nervous system upon the digestion, gland secretion and other functions of the body. Indeed, it has been demonstrated that the greater part of physical exhaustion is of emotional origin. The actual wear and tear of physical tissue caused by a hard day's work in an office is no more than that of a game of tennis, yet the one may cause exhaustion from the nervous tension caused by worry, fear, anxiety and other emotions, while the other will actually relax such tension and cause no consequent fatigue. Again, the technique for the culture of the emotions is practically the same, beginning with dissociation and analysis, and then proceeding by way of replacement or sublimation to the removal of the unwanted quality.

Above all, learn not to repress emotion. Emotion is force, however generated, and for all save the very few a force which is being produced each moment of the day. Such force obeys the law which applies to every form of energy, that if repressed it will, like a dammed up stream, find an outlet in some other way. Hence the 'complex' of modern psychology which often lies concealed beneath the phlegmatic calm of the Anglo-Saxon temperament. Many a 'nervous breakdown' is the final working out of such a knot in the sub-conscious, and all who have studied the pathology of fear, for example, know its devastating reaction both on body and mind.

In the meditation on the bodies the student learnt to say with some conviction, "I am not my emotions," and the same technique must be used with each one of them. Not until each emotion, be it fear or hatred, jealousy or sensuous desire, is dissociated from the meditator can it be replaced or sublimated. As already pointed out, one cannot remove from oneself what one believes to be a part of oneself, whereas to examine an emotion objectively is to remove its power to dominate the mind.

When the unwanted quality has been laid on the dissecting table by the process of dissociation, analyse its nature and, if possible, its psychological cause. As an aid to such analysis note how all emotion may be grouped under one of the two main forces, Love or Hate, using these terms to represent the contending forces of attraction and repulsion which hold the Universe in equilibrium. For these twin forces are complementary, and manifest in dual form on every plane. In physical science they may be seen, for example, in the laws of astronomy, dynamics, and electricity, while in engineering they appear as stress and strain. Even gravity, perhaps the best known natural force, is only half of a two-fold whole, for unless there were a force of repulsion as strong as gravity and acting in opposition to it, the Universe would be drawn into its centre and disappear. In the realm of emotion these principles manifest as love and hate, while in the realm of thought the same twin forces may be used for character building. It has been said that the laws of magnetism, which govern the interplay of these two fundamental forces, provide when truly understood a key to the working of the Universe, and those who hold that love is the guiding principle of life must remember that love, like any other principle, would be meaningless without its opposite.

Reference has already been made to the analogy between a moving stairway and cosmogenesis. Evolution implies a prior involution, and the two processes are in operation side by side. As man is on the ascending arc it follows that for him one set of forces are right and the other wrong. Thus, whereas selfishness is the law of matter, which is on the descending arc, selflessness is the law of spirit. In the same way love is right and hate is wrong, and to this extent love is indeed the law of our being. It follows that sooner or later we must not only cease to hate, but slay in ourselves the very capacity for hatred.

Above all, use the power of replacement to remove the most inhibiting of all emotions, fear, not only of individuals but of situations and events both present and yet to come. Courage is indeed the most essential quailty for spiritual development, for courage is the power which drives each weary pilgrim onward into the unknown. Fear shackles the feet of enterprise and, so those with psychic vision say, clings like a grey mist round the heart, and mind, inhibiting all action. Yet life is becoming, and spiritual life is a becoming more. No man can command success but any man may earn it, and the key lies in the one word Try. Who knows the limits of his powers until he tests them utterly?

Those emotions which are not easily replaced with complementary forces may be sublimated into higher forms. For love itself may manifest in many ways, from animal lust through earthly affection up to a force so sublimated that it is but the law of unity made manifest. Seen from this angle it is but another name for desire, which is in turn the directing force of will, for "Behind will stands desire". Yet this desire may be raised from selfish grasping to the unselfish will to service, and so to that same impersonal force which is the motive power of spirituality. Neither love nor desire nor any allied feeling can ever be stamped out, nor should we strive to slay them. Rather they should be deliberately raised in their objective until the lover and the loved, the desirer and the object of desire are merged in unity. Only in such a process will the voice of the personality begin to cry unheeded, and the springs of action begin to flow self-motived from within.

The Laws of Health

The greatest mind cannot function through a faulty instrument any more than a great violinist can fully manifest his genius through a poor violin. It follows that the physical body, being a necessary instrument of the mind, should be made and kept fit. But in order to control the body one must learn its laws, and a brief study of physiology and anatomy is most useful in the proper care of the body. Not only is the average person grossly ignorant of the functioning of his own mind, but he is equally ignorant of the mechanism of his own physical machine. Yet such elementary knowledge is as intensely interesting as it is easily acquired. Moreover, very little knowledge of anatomy and physiology will provide a wealth of material for meditation, the laws pertaining to the body being reflections of the laws of the Universe, which function on every plane.

The knowledge thus obtained will make it clear that the smooth functioning of the body depends mainly on the soundness of its structure and purity of the blood. First, the structure must be sound, for many discomforts and diseases are caused by a small displacement of some portion of the bony structure, usually the spine. Any competent osteopath will diagnose and cure such a displacement, thereby leaving nature free to remove the troubles caused by the structural injury.

But assuming that the structure as a whole is functioning freely, and assuming the absence of any organic

142

disease, health will depend mainly on the purity of the blood. Now the blood supply needs oxygen and certain chemicals. Oxygen is taken from the air; the chemicals are contained in food. Remember that the sole biological purpose of our many and varied meals is to supply the body with the raw materials with which it renews expended tissue and keeps itself at an even temperature. When too much food is taken there is an undue strain on the mechanism of elimination, and imperfect elimination of waste products leads inevitably to a host of troubles, ranging from a feeling of heaviness and fatigue to such apparently unconnected troubles as indigestion, rheumatism and catarrh.

The first rule of diet is therefore to halve the quantity. Most of us eat twice too much. It must never be forgotten that the actual quantity of chemicals needed daily is very small, and it follows that the purer the form in which they are taken, the less will be the bulk of useless matter to be passed through the digestive system and removed as waste. Reduce your meals, therefore, to two a day, and leave the table feeling you could comfortably eat more. There is much to be said for an occasional fast, or at least a 'fruit fast', that is, when nothing is eaten but a little fruit not more than twice a day.

The second rule is to balance the quantity, for too much or too little of any chemical will upset the chemical balance of the blood and in time affect the health. Most persons suffer from acidosis, yet a very little knowledge and trouble will remove this fruitful source of disease. If a vegetarian diet be preferred, let it be planned intelligently. A diet consisting solely of large quantities of cereals, ill-cooked vegetables and ill-chosen fruit will lack essential chemicals and strain the digestive mechanism. It is a sad fact that a large percentage of vegetarians suffer from indigestion, and many of them suffer abnormally from the cold. This is quite unnecessary provided that a little intelligent care be taken in the choice of food. The ideal diet avoids all rich and spicy foods or anything preserved or tinned. This is a difficult ideal, but very little thought will enable the average student at least to move towards it.

The third rule of diet is to avoid drinking at meals. When thirsty, and for no other reason, drink between meals, for drink with food dilutes the gastric juices and hinders the process of digestion. Avoid spirits and wines entirely, for alcohol makes higher meditation impossible. Those drinks in which the amount of alcohol in a single glass is negligible are on a par with smoking, and indulgence in such drugs as are contained in tea and coffee. If you can do without them, do without them; if not, be content for the moment with slowly reducing the amount consumed until the desire for them is dead.

Finally, remember that diet is essentially individual, for one man's meat is truly another man's poison. Experiment until you find what is best for you, but do not let your habits become too fixed. The perfectly trained body can eat anything at any time or go without. If you should be forced to eat what you do not like, or to overeat, do so cheerfully, and the next day eat nothing at all until nature has restored her equilibrium. Provided you do not violate a religious principle, it is far better to accommodate yourself to environment than to make yourself a nuisance to your friends and a laughing stock to those who are all too ready to judge a man by inessentials.

There remains the question of rest. Lack of rest produces strain, and strain produces of itself a host of troubles, leading ultimately to a breakdown of the machine.

The causes of strain are various. It may be that the body is being used too long at a time and allowed to sleep too little. Yet if it be not allowed sufficient sleep in which to repair the wastage of the day, a breakdown of the machine must ultimately follow, however long delayed. Another cause of strain is too much exercise. Certain nations have made a fetish of the need of exercise, and as a corollary look to muscular development as the test of health. It is nothing of the sort. Exercise, more than that incidental to the daily round, is quite unnecessary for the man whose diet is rational. If, however, the body is given twice the amount of food which is necessary for replacing used up tissue, it will feel the need of violent exercise to help it eliminate the excess. There is, however, much to be said for a few simple exercises night and morning in which to use those muscles which a sedentary life very seldom brings into play.

The subject of relaxation has already been treated in Part One of this manual, but the student is reminded that as meditation proceeds there will be an ever-increasing strain on the body which must be counterbalanced by periods of deliberate relaxation both of body and mind. In the early stages of concentration this strain was actually muscular, but the strain of higher meditation will manifest more subtly through the nerves. The student may find himself to his annoyance actually more irritable and hyper-sensitive. If this be so, and it is a common experience, remember that an increasing strain on any machine will inevitably find the flaws. Pay more attention to deep and rhythmic breathing, and purify the body in every way, in order that the progressive refinement of the instrument may keep pace with that of the mind.

Part Three

HIGHER MEDITATION

CHAPTER EIGHT

Higher Meditation

IT HAS been said that on the subject of Higher Meditation nothing useful can be written down. Yet words are
only symbols for ideas, and the greatest truths can be
expressed in symbol even though they be too great for
the concrete definitions so dear to the lower mind. This
language of symbol, of which words are the best form,
is common to all who tread the Path, and by its aid
the deeper mysteries of Reality may be glimpsed by all
who develop within themselves the ability to read the
meaning.

The dividing line between lower and higher meditation
is quite indefinite, such relative terms denoting succes-
sive stages of a continuous unfolding. But there comes a
time in the life of every student when a change occurs as
definite as it is indescribable. Those who try to describe
it use analogy which, though it cannot reveal the truth,
may yet, like a mirror, reflect it for the inward eye. To
some it seems as though the spiritual centre of gravity had
permanently shifted, producing a change of relative
values between the inner and the outer life. Henceforth
the inner life becomes the definite Reality, and the life of
the world but a pale reflection of that inner joy. Others
feel as a traveller who stands at the threshold of a new,
untrodden world, in which the limitations of unprofitable
thought are suddenly transcended, and things are seen for
the first time as they are. To other minds, again, the life-
force seems to change direction. Heretofore its flow was

outward, away from the heart of things, towards appearances; now it is inward, towards the heart of things, towards Reality.

If all this analogy seem fanciful, remember that the voice of mysticism speaks in a language of its own, and the truths of the inner life are better expressed in symbol, myth, and poetry than in the unimaginative accuracy of text-book terms. The latter may more clearly formulate the propositions of the lower mind; the former releases hidden springs of life and enables others to glimpse the flash of enlightenment which the inspired analogy or phrase enshrines. But by whatever analogy or phrase described, this new-found state of mind involves an irrevocable change. When once the inner eye is opened it can never again be closed. As a poet wrote on reaching this experience:

> "The future lies unmoulded in my hands.
>   A Path winds out before.
> There is no backward way. Behind me stands
>   A closéd door."

The new condition arrives suddenly, and the meditator finds himself in a dynamic silence whose limitations are immeasurable. There is a sense of latent power, of inward poise which calls up the analogy of an enormous flywheel, a condition of tremendous speed and power which is yet as silent as it is apparently motionless. This new experience is the connecting link between the habitual functioning of consciousness in the intellect and an equally habitual use of the intuition. Even in lower meditation the student began to use this higher faculty of direct cognition consciously, but as the higher levels of consciousness are deliberately entered, an experience which had been rare begins to become, if not habitual, at least more often and more easily used. The intellect builds up forms and uses them, but inevitably finds itself encompassed by the products of its own imagining. Only by the coming to flower of *Buddhi*, the faculty we know as the intuition, is the sense of separateness which form engenders, together with the limitations of those twin illusions, time and distance, slowly purged away. Yet this faculty is not the Self, for it is but a link between the intellect and Universal Mind which, so far from being a personal immortal soul, is as impersonal as the universal laws it represents. As is said in the *Lankavatara Sutra*, "Transcendental Intelligence rises when the intellectual-mind reaches its limit. If things are to be realized in their true nature, the processes of mentation, which are based on particularized ideas, discrimination and judgements, must be transcended by an appeal to some higher faculty of cognition, the intuitive-mind, which is a link between the intellectual-mind and the Universal Mind. While it is not an individualized organ like the intellectual-mind, it has that which is much better, direct dependence upon Universal Mind. While intuition does not give information that can be analysed and discriminated, it gives that which is far superior, self-realisation through indentification."

At first this faculty, whose voice is paradox, appears in occasional flashes of *satori*, momentary enlightenment, but as time goes on the quantity and quality of these moments is gradually extended until its 'heatless light'

irradiates each moment of the day. The effect is fundamental. No longer does the student act from conscious
choice of two alternatives, but chooses right because
right-doing has become ingrained in character. Henceforth the choice is automatic, for the student acts in
obedience to an inner law, and knows full well the
penalties of disobedience. This inner prompting is now
the student's sole 'authority'; henceforth he leans on no
man, having learnt to stand alone. In the language of
mysticism he neither seeks nor treads the Path—he
becomes it. As it said in *The Voice of the Silence*, "Thou
canst not travel on the Path before thou hast become that
Path itself."

This inward revolution has a disturbing effect on the
intellect and on the day's routine. Matters of little moment
now become of prime importance, and principles thought
fundamental are found to be a hindrance to be cast away.
Pleasures that once attracted now grow tedious; study
and thought that once seemed wearisome now clamour for
time. The student finds that study which entails the use
of intuition actually releases force instead of using it, and
meditation rouses dormant energy which leaves him far
more vital than before. There is, however, the inevitable
price to pay for such advancement. Habits of speech and
action must now be far more rigorously controlled. A
promise, however lightly given, and whether to oneself
or another, must be scrupulously kept. Be careful, therefore, of the lightest undertaking or resolve. In the same
way each of the Precepts must be lived on a higher level.
The student must live up, for example, to a far higher
standard of truthfulness, and respect for life must be

interpreted as abstaining from any thought as well as act
which is inimical to the evolution of other forms of consciousness.

The Abandonment of Intellect

The most upsetting change, however, is that which
follows the abandonment of the very intellect which years
and lives of effort had developed and controlled, the very
thought-machine by which the new-found state of
consciousness had been attained. Yet, to quote once more
from that classic of self-development, *The Voice of the
Silence*, "The Mind is the greater Slayer of the Real. Let
the Disciple slay the Slayer." All would be well if this
could be accomplished at one blow, but the task is long
and wearisome. It is one thing to realise, as stated by
Porphyry, that "of that nature which is beyond intellect
many things are asserted according to intellection, but it
is contemplated by a cessation of intellectual energy better
than with it"; it is quite another to accommodate one's
mind to a state in which the god of reason is triumphantly
dethroned. Here is a world as puzzling to the student as
the change within him may be to his friends. Logic and
reason are the architects which build the hovels or
palaces of intellectual thought; the intuition rises above
the world of forms into the world of Being, and the
builders of forms are accordingly left behind. Good sense
is no longer the sole criterion of a proposition's truth or
falsity, for the higher mind may see that what is nonsense
to the thought-bound scholar is in fact magnificently true.
It has been flippantly said that a paradox is a truth standing on its head to attract attention; certain principles

are undoubtedly best expressed in this irrational form. Yet, as will be seen in a later chapter on Zen methods of meditation, this release from the domination of the intellect goes further than mere paradox, and the whimsical and joyous irrelevance of Zen *Mondo* (questions and answers) can drive the proudly rational mind into despair. Certain it is that no man should go further into meditation who has not found within himself a faculty superior to the thinking mind.

But whether for this reason or for some other, let those who feel no urgent call for further spiritual adventures read no more. The 'Doctrine of the Eye' is always available for the many; the 'Doctrine of the Heart' was ever for the few. "Yet", as *The Voice of the Silence* urges, "if the 'Doctrine of the Heart' is too high-winged for thee . . . be warned in time: remain content with the 'Eye Doctrine' of the Law. Hope still. For if the 'Secret Path' is unattainable this 'day', it is within thy reach 'to-morrow', " that is, in lives to come. If the decision be taken to go forward, look once more to the motive that prompted the resolve. Powers may come to you upon the journey, and visions of Truth ever nearer Pure Enlightenment. Yet these are not your aim. There is but one right motive for this pilgrimage, the enlightenment of all mankind. Unless this pure compassion be the mainspring of all future effort the Path is best forgotten, for any less desire will only strengthen the illusion of separateness, and thus defer the day when separation finds reunion.

Subjects of Higher Meditation

In the early stages of any art or science it is not merely possible but almost necessary to lay down a definite course of graded exercises in order to lead the student by easy stages up to conscious mastery. As the higher levels are reached, however, the personal predispositions and preferences of the individual begin to manifest, and it becomes increasingly difficult to suggest, much less to impose a line of further progress suitable to all. What applies to the more mundane arts and sciences applies still more to the spiritual science of meditation, for no two persons bring over from past lives the same tendencies, abilities, and chosen field of work.

In choosing a subject for higher meditation it will be found that the nature of the subject is of less importance than the level at which it is reviewed. For example, one may meditate on the Buddha as a man, a spiritual Teacher or a cosmic principle, the difference lying not in the subject but in the meditator's mind. The explanation lies in the fact that the path of progress is an upward spiral and not a straight line. It follows that the same complete circuit is trodden again and again, but at each revolution one arrives at the same point though at a higher level. Thus the highest spiritual experiences may be at least partially understood by the humblest student, for all the stages from deepest ignorance to pure enlightenment are trodden again and again upon the spiral journey, at each revolution the darkness growing less profound and the enlightenment more glorious. Each one who strives to meditate has already left the world, tried all known methods of vicarious salvation, turned within, been sorely tempted, found enlightenment and shared it with the world, only to succumb once more, though never so completely, to the lure of the senses. The Great Renunciation will not face one for the first time at the journey's end, for we are making it each moment of the day. In the same way every stage of the Path is being constantly retrodden, yet slowly one ascends the mountain side. It is true that there are those who seem to move in a mere circle, and it may be that these are they who, failing to profit by experience, repeat the errors of the past on returning to the same point of the cycle, and so slip back to the position they had reached before. Those who know the game of 'Snakes and Ladders' will find that it illustrates a mighty law.

Applying these principles, it will be found that subjects used in lower meditation may be used again; the difficulties, triumphs and temptations of the past lying dormant until the cycle returns. This law of cycles being one of the basic principles of the Universe is itself a valuable subject for meditation, for with the help of analogy it will enable the student to understand as never before the laws which operate in nature and in man, and the mechanism of that process of becoming by which both are moving slowly towards their essential identity.

Return, then, to the subjects already used, yet examine them from a higher point of view. For example, the meditation on the bodies may be used again, but having dissociated consciousness from the lower principles of body, emotions and thought, the student should try to raise still further the level upon which he still thinks 'I am I'. The same applies to the meditation on 'Things as they are.' Pass from a merely intellectual examination of their essential nature to the life of which they are the outward form. The subject of Self, again, is of course inexhaustible, and of such importance that it will be considered in its higher aspects at a later stage.

Loosening the Fetters of Form

Meditation upon all these subjects will be immensely aided by the employment of the newly-developed faculty of intuition. As already pointed out, this is not so much a new vehicle of consciousness as a light which illumines the higher mind. Its use will help the student to overcome the ingrained habits of form-building which is the work of the lower mind. It is all too easy to force the plastic substance of one's thought into conformity with a chosen and admired ideal, but this destroys the mind's intrinsic pliability, and the purpose of meditation is not to conform to the chosen subject but to extract from it whatever truth it contains and manifest that truth in character. As the range of subject is ever widening, the mind must become increasingly adaptable, resisting the quality of inertia which ever strives to hold it within the limits of some agreeable form. Speaking of human consciousness to-day, Miss Geraldine Coster says in *Yoga and Western Psychology:* "People ask that life shall be absolute in values, and shall not take them unawares. Relativity, however, is of the essence of life. Life moves, changes inevitably, and the unexpected and the unknown are always coming upon us. Owing to ignorance there is in every man a deep resistance to life as life, an incapacity to accept the flow of things and adapt to it freely. It is sitting loose to life, accepting it as it comes rather than demanding from it what you expect that both analyst and yogi regard as constituting the 'free psyche', 'liberation', which in the eyes of both is the pearl of great price worth any sacrifice to attain." After all, the loftiest concepts are only mind-made forms for expressing spiritual truths, and, as every Buddhist knows, all forms are perishable. Our goal is nothing less than that very Enlightenment which is the soul of form. As is written in the *Sutra of Hui Neng*, "Our Essence of Mind is intrinsically pure; all things, good or evil, are only its manifestations, and good deeds and evil deeds are only the result of good thoughts and evil thoughts respectively." And again, "When we are free from attachment to all outer objects, the mind will be in peace. Our Essence of Mind is intrinsically pure, and the reason why we are perturbed is simply because we allow ourselves to be carried away by the very circumstances we are under. He who is able to keep his mind unperturbed, irrespective of circumstances, has real *Samadhi*." The increasing range of spiritual vision afforded by the development of the faculty of *Buddhi* thus loosens the bonds which fetter the mind to forms, and assists the student to consider concepts as aspects of truth, irrespective of the form in which they happen to manifest. What is needed by the student of Higher Meditation is not ever more spiritual concepts with which to exercise his power of abstract thought, but ever deeper and deeper spiritual experience. Concepts are a necessary means of mental communication, but they are no substitute for personal experience of the truths they only partially reveal.

As is written in the *Lankavatara Sutra*: "Then said Mahamati to the Blessed One: Why is it that the ignorant are given up to discrimination and the wise are not?"

The Blessed One replied: "It is because the ignorant cling to names, signs and ideas; as their minds move along these channels they feed on multiplicities of objects and fall into the notion of an ego-soul and what belongs to it; they make discriminations of good and bad among appearances and cling to the agreeable. As they thus cling there is a reversion to ignorance, and karma, born of greed, anger and folly is accumulated. As the accumulation of karma goes on they become imprisoned in a cocoon of discrimination and are thenceforth unable to free themselves from the round of birth and death."

Until the student can overcome this 'cocoon of discrimination' in thought and speech he will never attain that self-realisation of which the Sutra speaks at a later stage. "Self-realisation is an exalted state of inner attainment which transcends all dualistic thinking and is above the mind system with its logic, reasoning, theorising and illustrations." If this seems difficult, remember that sooner or later the mind must be led to an understanding that *all* forms, including the Universe itself, are mind-begotten, being children of the Universal Mind. To quote again from the *Lankavatara Sutra*, the Blessed One, asked to explain wherein lay the error of certain philosophers, replied, "The error lies in this, that they do not recognise that the objective world rises from the mind itself, that the whole mind system also rises from the mind itself; but depending upon these manifestations of the mind as being real they go on discriminating them, cherishing the dualism of this and that, of being and non-being, ignorant of the fact that there is but one common Essence." Yet, while contemplating the heights of consciousness as yet unwon, it is well to remember that the Real and the Unreal are but relative terms to our present consciousness. As Dr Jung points out in his commentary on *The Secret of the Golden Flower*, "Obviously, the veil of *Maya* cannot be lifted by a mere decision of reason, but demands the most thorough-going and wearisome preparation consisting in the right payment of all debts to life. For as long as one is in any way held by the domination of *cupiditas*, the veil is not lifted, and the heights of a consciousness, empty of content and free of illusion, are not reached, nor can any trick nor any deceit bring it about."

For the moment one may begin by trying to eliminate the use of words in meditation. It is hard to escape the habit of formulating to oneself in words an experience which pertains to a realm above the intellect. Yet the moment one tries to clothe in words, even to oneself, a genuine spiritual experience, the sense of reality is gone, and one is left with a pale shadow of its splendour clothed in the worn-out garments of our daily thought. Begin by trying to think of simple things without the use of the words by which we habitually describe them, and then pass on to ideas. This dissociation of thought from language is at all times difficult, but particularly so to Westerners, whose concrete minds are generally bound by labels, definitions and outward forms. Try, for example, when meditating on the bodies, to raise the consciousness through the various vehicles without actually saying to yourself, "I am not my body, emotions, mind—these are not I," and in the same way in the *Brahma Viharas* pour out loving-kindness and the rest without using those terms or thinking of their names. This exercise will help the mind to form the habit of seeing all things as they essentially are, without reference to the label which at that moment they may happen to bear.

CHAPTER NINE

The Raising of Consciousness

THE NEXT step is to begin the deliberate raising of consciousness. The process is dual, a raising of the consciousness in meditation to heights hitherto unreached, and a corresponding raising of the habitual level during the whole of the waking day. The student must at the same time learn to draw up every form of the life-force which has hitherto functioned mainly at lower levels, and express it at a higher point of the spiral. Thus sex, which is but a physical manifestation of the creative force, must be raised from the physical to the equivalent creative centre in the mind. This 'transformation of seed into power', as it is called in the *Secret of the Golden Flower*, is the process by which those who have detached themselves from the sway of the senses produce the creative energy required for 'crossing the stream', that is, the rebirth of the personal into the impersonal. Hence the foolishness, for it is no more nor less, of wasting this force in unproductive ways. To quote again from the same work: "The fool wastes the most precious jewel of his body in uncontrolled pleasures and does not know how to conserve the power of his seed. When it is finished the body perishes. The Holy and Wise men have no other way of taking care of their lives except by destroying lusts and safeguarding the seed." For the seed is the source of power, and when transmuted into higher forms provides the dynamic flow of life in which to move towards enlightenment.

In the new condition of consciousness once more review the self, and see with clearer eyes how most of our difficulties arise from thinking of ourselves as separated units, whereas "the notion that our little life is a separate independent unit, fighting for its own hand against countless separate independent units, is a delusion of the most tormenting kind. So long as we thus see the world and life, peace broods far off on an inaccessible pinnacle. When we feel and know that all selves are one, then peace of mind is ours without any fear of loss." (Besant, *Thought Power*.) So long as we have this 'fear of loss' we may know that we still cling to the Great Heresy, the existence of a separated self. Only when the fetters of this illusion begin to fall will the pilgrim begin to see that in "Forgoing self the Universe grows I."

Having learnt that to one whose intuition is awakened the voice of paradox is clearer than any reasoned argument, the student may return to the mighty saying, "I am not yet I am." Here, in the minimum of words, will be found the alternative paths to self-perfection, to slay the Not-Self or to become the Self. The Southern School of Buddhism prefers the former, Indian philosophy stresses the latter, while Mahayana Buddhism combines the two. As already pointed out, whether one says of the lower, separative, personal self, "This is not I," or of the spiritual, impersonal, Universal Self, "I am," is surely a matter for each student to decide. Whether the selfish, grasping 'I' be so reduced by meditation and self-discipline that it no longer offers resistance to the flow of cosmic life, or whether the higher, spiritual self be so progressively expanded that in the end it is commensurate with all

Creation, is surely a matter of choice and not of argument. Yet more unkindness and lack of understanding have arisen over this pair of opposites than any other doctrine save the nature of Reality. Wherefore meditate once more upon that mighty saying, "I am not yet I am". There is, however, a subtle danger in cultivating the Self. The East knows the meaning of Self too well to fall into the trap, but the West, as yet in its spiritual infancy, may fail to distinguish sufficiently between the higher and lower aspects of our complex being, and glorify the personality instead of the impersonal Life-Force which is no man's property, and thus produce instead of greater selflessness an overwhelming egotism. Herein lies the value of the method so strongly advocated by the Southern School, of systematically denying selfhood to the lower vehicles, by which method, even though it be one-sided, the taint of egotism is not only avoided but more easily removed.

The Meditation on the 'Higher Third'

The solution to the paradox of self, however, will never be found by merely regarding such pairs of opposites as complementary. This superficial view has led to a serious misunderstanding of the Buddha's doctrine of the Middle Way. As Dr Barua pointed out in a lecture on the "*Universal Aspect of Buddhism*" (*Maha-Bodhi Journal*, July, 1934), "When two so-called finalities or ultimate truths come into conflict with each other, as *asti* with *nasti*, there must necessarily be a 'third' (tertium quid) to unify them in meaning without being identified with either. Buddha's term to denote this 'third' is *majjha* (*madhya*) which in later nomenclature took rather the misleading form of *majjhima patipada*, generally rendered 'Middle Path'. "

This tertium quid, or synthesis of duality, forms the apex of a triangle, thus producing stability out of tension. It is at once independent of, yet arising from the correlative opposites, and forms with them a trinity which is the metaphysical basis for all the Trinities found in every religion and philosophy, and indeed wherever there is a pair of antitheses in relationship. But a more perfect understanding of the triangle is achieved by reviewing the apex as the source rather than as the synthesis of the two correlatives. Remember that the Life-force is One in essence, yet manifests as the duality of Spirit-matter, life-form, light and darkness, good and evil, male-female, and so through all the derived antitheses which form the manifested Universe. But duality as such can never exist alone, for there is always a third factor in the relationship between them. (Compare the third aspect of *karma*, which is at once cause, effect, and the relation between the two.) This relationship is merely a lower reflection of the unity from which the two opposing factors spring. Thus all dualities are really trinities, and the trinity is but a threefold aspect of the One. As is written in the *Sutra of Hui Neng*, "Buddhism is known as having no two ways. There are good ways and evil ways, but since Buddha-nature is neither, therefore Buddhism is known as having no two ways. . . . The nature of non-quality is Buddha-nature." Add to this another passage, "Doubt not that Buddha is within your own mind, apart from which nothing can exist," and the intuitive student will find a clue to the nature of that Self which is above duality.

The need of the intuition is here imperative. No paradox of opposing opposites can ever be resolved at its own level. One *must* rise in consciousness to a plane from which both correlatives are seen as functions of a third. It is true that most of us cannot yet contact the Essence of mind, but remembering the laws of the spiral, and letting the light of intuition illumine the meditating mind, one can at least perceive the tremendous possibilities afforded by an understanding of this subtle truth, and learn how to act accordingly.

To quote again from Dr. Barua: "Interpreted in this light, Buddhism is to be considered a mode of life which is neither a mere half-hearted compromise between, nor a mere studied evasion of, two extremes. It must have such an independent movement of its own as to be able to make the rest moving or dynamic." In the same way the mind of the student must have an independent movement of its own in which to resolve each paradox and pair of opposites. In a word, the Middle Way lies not so much between as *above* extremes. The lower viewpoint all too easily becomes a feeble compromise instead of that dynamic pressing forward, that ever becoming more by which the fearless Pilgrim, as he learns to 'become the Path itself,' finds all extremes restored to a higher unity within his own advanced mind.

What, then, is the nature of this synthetic factor we have called the 'higher third?' The answer will vary with the level of consciousness. That which includes both selfish and altruistic motives, for example, is the perfect motive which seems to us an absence of motive. Again, that which is higher than good and evil as popularly understood is a higher Good which moves on levels far above conventional morality. But as we move up the mountain side we shall find that the pairs of opposites are manifesting on a correspondingly higher level, for they are in a way but outposts of the mind. It follows that the higher third will seem to evolve correspondingly, until we reach in time a position where the supreme antitheses which appear as complementary cosmic forces know no higher synthesis than the Absolute which includes them all. Once more apply the analogy of the spiral and strive to understand, for a grasp of this principle is as necessary as it is difficult.

The Search for the Impersonal

Applying these principles to the subject of self, the student will find that the paradox of the Self and the Not-Self can only be solved from the viewpoint of a unifying third. This doctrine certainly applies in resolving the conflicts which torment the psychologically unsound. In his Commentary on *The Secret of the Golden Flower*, Dr Jung, in speaking of the conflict between the conscious and the unconscious, says: "I always worked with the temperamental conviction that in the last analysis there are no insoluble problems, and experience has so far justified me in that I have often seen individuals who simply outgrew a problem which had destroyed others. This 'out-growing' revealed itself on further experience to be the raising of the level of consciousness. Some higher or wider interest arose on the person's horizon, and through this widening of his view the insoluble problem lost its urgency. It was not solved logically in its own terms, but faded out in contrast to a new and stronger life-tendency. It was not repressed and made unconscious, but merely appeared in a different light, and so became different itself." This applies equally to the warfare in the conscious mind between the dissociated aspects of the self, the "higher and wider interest" being that of an impersonal point of view. Thus speaks *The Voice of the Silence*: "Seek in the Impersonal for the 'Eternal Man', and having sought him out, look inward: thou art Buddha." It is true that we cannot at once become completely impersonal, but we may rise so far up the spiral that we reach a point at which we are sufficiently above the conflict to unite its opposing views. To achieve the impersonal point of view, realise that the true Self, that is to say, the truest Self that you can become, is not the actor in the world of action. "He who seeth that all his actions are performed by nature only, and that the self within is not the actor, sees indeed." (*Bhagavad Gita*.) In the words of *Light on the Path*, "Stand aside in the coming battle, and though thou fightest be not thou the warrior." The secret of this attitude is the Taoist doctrine of *wu wei*, "sitting loose of life," as Miss Coster calls it, a position of detachment in which the twin forces of attraction and aversion are held in equilibrium. Learn to objectivise still more the functioning of the lower vehicles, remembering that one cannot control anything which one still regards as part of oneself. Dissociate the consciousness from undesirable elements in the mind, while still preserving a sense of the oneness and wholeness of the Self. Yet see that the process is one of dissociation and not repression. "Disciples sometimes think that they can expedite the attainment of their goal of tranquillization by entirely suppressing the activities of the mind system. This is a mistake, for even if the activities of the mind are suppressed, the mind will still go on functioning because the seeds of habit-energy will still remain in it." (*Lankavatara Sutra*.)

The secret of action in inaction and of inaction in action, described at length in the *Bhagavad Gita*, is a delicate balance between positive and negative, between the over-use of force which will precipitate action and its consequent *karma*, and the insufficient self-exertion which may leave one stranded on the sand-bank while the flow of life goes by. On the one hand we are warriors striving towards self-liberation from the thraldom of illusion; on the other hand, we are preparing ourselves as conduit pipes or channels through which the waters of life may pass with unimpeded flow. The centre point between these attitudes can only be attained by removing the ego-centric point of view, for these are they who "stand in their own shadows and wonder why it is dark".

On the all-important subject of self, then, it will be seen that the paradoxes in which the truth lies buried, such as "I am not yet I am", will only yield their secret to a higher point of view which unifies the opposites. Once this impersonal position is attained one may learn to watch as a dispassionate spectator the interplay of the natural forces which we fondly imagine to be the products of our will.

The Three Gunas

In order to achieve the impersonal point of view above the pairs of opposites, a state of right action wherein the actor is unconcerned with the fruits of action, the student is advised to study the three qualities of matter called in Indian philosophy the Gunas, who interaction weaves the complex pattern of the manifested Universe. The characteristics, *tamas, rajas, sattva* are variously translated, for they may be viewed from many aspects. *Tamas,* the lowest of the trinity, may be translated inertia, *rajas* in this connection being force, activity, motion, and *sattva* the quality of balance or harmony which unifies the two. Other readings of the trinity are illusion, action and illumination, or ignorance, desire and truth. Again, one may regard *tamas* as the condition where one cannot discriminate between the pairs of opposites, *rajas* as the stage when one over-discriminates and separates, and *sattva* as the synthesis of the separated pairs.

In the light of the doctrine of the Higher Third one may regard *rajas* and *tamas* as the positive and negative qualities in nature respectively, and *sattva* as the unifying third, but however viewed, the three principles form an interlocked triangle, each one partaking of the others' qualities, and between them including every phase of activity. The mind itself is no exception to the rule, and as the *gunas* are really the forces of form, their constant interaction tends to fetter consciousness to its lower vehicles, whatever the unit of consciousness may be. Each of the forces binds according to its nature, *tamas* through indifference and laziness, *rajas* through *karma* which springs from action prompted by desire, and *sattva* itself by attaching the mind to the pleasure which the quality of *sattva* brings. It follows that only as we learn to detach our consciousness from its lower vehicles, that is, to learn that it is not *our* consciousness at all, can we achieve the impersonal, dispassionate viewpoint of the Middle Way. Yet in success along this path is found the normal development of the *siddhis*, those super-normal powers which foolish persons seek to develop in order to satisfy their personal desires. For as the mind itself is a product of the *gunas*, being of the world of form, it follows that control of the mind will prepare the way for control of other manifestations of the qualities, including those forces of nature by whose aid the *siddhis* operate. Hence the mysterious powers of telepathy, clairvoyance, levitation and the like whose secret lies in the fundamental identity of force and matter, and of the forces of nature with those of the mind.

A glance at the relative function of the three *gunas* in certain spheres of activity will show that *sattva* is the balancing third which unifies extremes. To quote from the 18th chapter of the *Bhagavad Gita*, "Know that the wisdom which perceives in all nature one single principle is of the *sattva* quality. The knowledge which perceives different and manifold principles as present in the world pertains to *rajas*, but that knowledge which is attached to one object alone as if it were the whole is of the nature of *tamas*." Again speaking of action, "The action which is right, performed without attachment to results, free from pride and selifishness, is of the *sattva* quality. That is of *rajas* which is done with a view to its consequences, or with great exertion, or with egotism. And that which in consequence of delusion is done without regard to consequences or the power to carry it out, or the harm it may cause, is of the quality of darkness, *tamas*."

The personality, however, is so bound by the qualities that a position where *sattva* rules is not easy to attain, and a level of consciousness where even *sattva* is seen as a quality of matter is still more difficult. Yet from the heights of the impersonal the student may watch, serene, detached and yet compassionate, the interplay of the qualities in his own personality and in the manifested world around. Here is the field of battle in which the opposites wage war, and he is wise indeed who learns to perform all action so impersonally and with such indifference to reward that his consciousness is never entangled in the conflict of the dualities, but remains at all times in the "imperturbability of the Essence of Mind".

The Voice of Mysticism

Those to whom a sense of the individuality of all apparently divided things is a live and wonderful reality need no intellectual argument to support their knowledge of the Self's essential unity. Though their feet be still of clay, their eyes have seen the light reflected from Enlightenment, and though the vision be above description save in a richly coloured symbolism common to them all, yet they *know* as a spiritual experience truths which can never be understood with the cumbrous mechanism of the intellectual mind.

This does not mean that the mystic can avoid the warfare of the selves, but that his method of dealing with the problem is fundamentally different. To him the sense of wholeness is paramount, and the finer aspect of his mind is solely concerned with the renunciation of everything which stands between him and the All of which he never ceases to feel himself a part. Whether his symbolism be that of fire, as the flame which seeks absorption in the Sun, of water, as of the drop which slips into the Shining Sea, or of love, as the lover who yearns for the Beloved, the feeling is the same—and indescribable. The greatest English poem upon the subject is Francis Thompson's *Hound of Heaven*, and the same insistence on the all-pervading Presence of the Beloved is found in Tennyson's poem, *The Higher Pantheism*—"Closer is He than breathing, and nearer than hands and feet."

Yet there is nothing personal in such a relationship, for the 'Beloved,' whether viewed as Krishna, Christ or Buddha, is the same impersonal 'God within', whose nature is that Essence of Mind which is above all differences. This constant sense of unity, of wholeness with all life, leads in some to a fierce impatience, amounting sometimes to intolerance of all forms and organizations and even of formulated ideas. Yet life and form are only another of the pairs of opposites, and life cannot manifest without its form. Herein lies a trap for the unwary, well expressed in a Chinese saying: "To him who knows nothing of Buddhism, mountains are mountains and trees are trees. To him who knows a little of Buddhism, mountains are no longer mountains and trees no longer trees. But when he becomes enlightened, mountains are once more mountains and trees are trees." All of us know the first stage, for it is that everyday experience, but there comes a time when all things are seen anew and in fresh relationship. Dazzled with a fleeting glimpse of something they assume to be Reality, some students speak complacently of knowing the Self as One, of having slain the desires of self, of being reabsorbed into the Light. In plain fact, they have attained a fleeting experience of *satori*, a momentary irradiation of the lower self with the light of *Buddhi*, and it is an experience, assuming it to be genuine, which none can easily forget. But there is a higher stage, at which mountains are once more seen as mountains and trees as trees, and the spiritual experience is known for what it is. Yet there will be this difference, that the student will henceforth know that, though unquestionably different in form, these trees and mountains and all other manifested things are divers aspects and expressions of one Life, to be viewed accordingly. A good example is the comparison of religions. Most students begin by considering their own the best, which may be true—for them. Later, they study the Wisdom of which all religions are but a partial expression, and somewhat hastily announce that all religions are one and there is no difference between them. Yet the time comes when they begin to see that the differences between religions are, in sober fact, enormous, and so, while appreciating that their widely differing doctrines are so many distorted aspects of one unvarying truth, they once more observe that mountains are mountains and trees are trees.

The Fullness and the Void

Those who have risen to some extent above the world of name and form will find the heart expanding to receive a thousand aspects of the truth which prejudice had hitherto concealed. For such new visitors we must needs make room in the 'Cave of the Heart', for as Mr Cranmer-Byng points out in the *Vision of Asia*, "all men and works, whether of men or God, come into our understanding through this capacity of making room. It is a capacity for expansion and containing. Expansion through growth, containing through space. The microcosm of man approaches the macrocosm of God through fullness of life and experience, through knowledge acquired and works accomplished. But it also approaches Him through emptiness, through its power to cast out whatever is useless or redundant, through the space that it makes within itself for the incoming of the tidal waters of life. Thought is both fluid and tidal. It flows outward from us into the world of life and is expressed in waves of rhythm, in tumult of discord, in billows of passion, in ripples of laughter, and, at rare moments, in wordless depths of feeling. And life surging without and around us gives back in full measure according to our capacity to make room and receive." Some students who have reached an appreciation of this tide of life complain of a sense of fullness of new understanding which, though a source of joy, yet shatters their peace of mind. They do not realize that an equanimity so easily disturbed is not of the substance of eternity, and is no loss. Others, and they are more common, speak of a feeling of emptiness, of a constantly increasing vacuum which is as constantly refilled. Here the student who has meditated on the self will perceive the dual process of attainment, that of becoming more and more the Self or less and less the Not-Self, reflected in his mind. Whether one grows by a sense of fullness which slowly fills the Universe, or by an ever-increasing vacuum which merges in the Void, the result is the same—and indescribable.

Taoists know that of the two opposites space is more valuable, as the following quotation from Okakura, taken from the *Vision of Asia*, testifies: "Lao Tzu claimed that only in vacuum lay the truly essential. The reality of a room, for instance, was to be found in the vacant space enclosed by the roof and walls themselves. Vacuum is all potent because all containing. In vacuum alone motion becomes possible. One who could make of himself a vacuum into which others might enter would become master of all situations." There is deep psychological value in this final phrase. The man who can without hesitation accept each circumstance and absorb it into himself has robbed it of its power to affect his mind. This involves a considerable degree of selflessness, and the ability to crush out instantly all emotional reaction of like or dislike, together with all thoughts of consequences, good or evil, to oneself. The happening, grave or trivial, must be seen for what it is, yet instantly *accepted*. All intervening processes of thought must be at once dropped, for the erection of such barriers at the doors of mind prevents an entrance into the vacuum above described. This instantaneous acceptance stifles at birth all trace of worry, hope or fear, and is a long step on the road to the control of circumstances, for henceforth between oneself and the circumstance no feeling of duality is permitted to arise.

The same applies to one's attitude to other individuals.

On meeting a fellow being there is an instantaneous reaction of like or dislike, and an equally spontaneous mental criticism. Try to eliminate this reaction, and *accept* this other aspect of yourself, either by using the mystical technique of feeling that he, too, is part of the all-embracing wholeness, or the more rational method of contacting him at the highest level of consciousness which you can reach, at which exalted level the personality, which roused such fierce reaction, does not exist. In any event raise no fresh barriers, but draw this other 'spark of the Flame' into your heart, and know yourselves as one.

CHAPTER TEN

The Doctrine of the Act

THE PRACTICE of 'acceptance,' itself by no means easy, is akin to another still more difficult, which possibly no words can adequately describe. Yet the hints which follow, themselves obtained in meditation, may help the intuitive student to grasp the principles involved.

It is clear that the mind has two aspects, the lower, concrete thought-machine reflecting the higher, more impersonal and abstract intellect. It should be equally clear to the thoughtful student that the feelings and emotions are a lower aspect of the Self than the mind and yet reflect a higher faculty, the intuition. Assuming these premises, and they are the fruits of serious investigation, there remain two aspects of our being uncollated, the highest and the lowest, being the extremes of Spirit and Matter repectively. The fundamental relationship between these two triangles may easily be reduced to diagram form, the higher trinity composed of (1) the Life-principle itself, which is no man's exclusive property, (2) Buddhi, the faculty of intuition which illumines (3) the higher, abstract mind. The lower triangle, which represents the compound personality, consists of (1) the thought-machine which at present dominates Western psychology, (2) the feelings and emotions which reflect, and often claim to be the intuition, and (3) the body which is the instrument of consciousness on the physical plane. But if two of the three points of the triangles are reflected in their correspondences, why not the third? Surely reason insists that the body is the direct reflection of Spirit, the most limited and finite vehicle reflecting the limitless and infinite? Meditation upon this discovery brings many corroborative quotations to mind. For example, where are we to seek the purely impersonal save in this garment of the personality? "Within thy body— the shrine of thy sensations—seek in the Impersonal for the 'Eternal Man', and having sought him out, look inward: thou art *Buddha*." (*The Voice of the Silence*.) Christ in the same way speaks of the body as the temple of the Spirit, while physiologists and anatomists with thoughts above the purely material have found in this vehicle of humble matter a Universe in miniature.

The suggested correspondence is the meeting of extremes, yet it is a paradoxical axiom that extremes will always meet. The phrase has many meanings, but one will here suffice. If two men try to get as far away from one another as possible by travelling East and West respectively they will sooner or later meet. Meditate on this, even though it involves the circularity of the Universe, for you will have the most modern scientists to support the timeless wisdom of the East, in which the Unmanifest is always symbolised as a 'circle centreless'. Spirit and matter are in essence One, and the extremes reflect each other. If this be so, and only in meditation can the individual know that it is so, then action, the expression of consciousness on the physical plane, is a direct reflection of the creative aspect of the pure Life-principle.

All this may sound mere abstract metaphysics, but these principles have tremendous bearing on the humblest act, as on our attitude to life in general, for they prove the fundamental teaching of the All-Enlightened One that life must be lived to the uttermost before it can be cast away. This is the central message of the Dhamma, to conquer life by living it, not by striving to escape from that which is yourself in another form. No aspect of the Self can reach perfection until the Self as a whole is perfected, and as the wholeness of each self is indissolubly entwined with every other aspect of the Universe, it follows that Life must move along the Path of Becoming as a single unit—or not at all. The implications of this discovery ripple out beyond the confines of description. Here is the heart of the tremendous saying: "There is no such thing as sacrifice; there is only opportunity to serve." All sacrifice, from the littlest act of self-denying charity up to the Great Renunciation itself is equally inevitable, for to claim self-liberation while there remains one blade of grass not yet enlightened is to leave that one black dot within the golden circle of enlightenment. Herein lies the spiritual tragedy of those who strive for self-liberation without the motive of doing so the better to enlighten all mankind. Such persons truly reach enlightenment, only to find in it the sentence of their own damnation, for the self they have saved is their own self, and between them and the Wholeness they must one day consciously re-enter lies a gulf of suffering which few men have attempted to describe.

The Dhamma, then, is a way of living, not a way of escape from life, a way of right action in which each aspect of the Self, from highest to lowest, is fused in conscious unity. It follows that Buddhist Meditation, so far from being "escapist" in its aim, is a positive, dynamic method for achieving this self-synthesis.

Then what is the perfect act? It may be described as the right man using the right means at the right time and without motive, an 'action purposeless'. Consider these factors separately. There is the right man for each act. As the *Bhagavad Gita* points out clearly, there is danger in another's duty, and the wise man does not lightly assume responsibility until he is satisfied that it is rightly his. On the other hand, it is equally unwise to shirk responsibility offered for one's acceptance, for it is a sound principle that when a task presents itself as needing doing it is right to do it unless a more suitable person intervenes. The wise man follows the middle way between the two extremes, neither desiring nor repelled by action, but acting as occasion requires, impersonally.

It is pointed out in *The Secret of the Golden Flower* that if "the wrong man uses the right means, the right means work in the wrong way". It is equally true that if the right man uses the wrong means he will be wasting power and possibly producing troublesome consequences. Experience alone will teach the student what is in all the circumstances the right means of action, and though at first the choice involves a conscious deliberation, the time will come when in the perfect act the choice is unerring and instantaneous.

Most thinkers know that time is an illusion, but we live in a world of relative values, and to our limited consciousness the changing panorama of manifestation appears as an ordered sequence, as a constant flow. As is said by the Buddhist Lama in Talbot Mundy's *Om*,

"Time is a delusion. All is the eternal Now. But in a world in which all is a delusion, of which time is a controlling element, there is a proper time for all things. We cannot mount the camel that has passed us, nor the camel that has not yet come." This is the true interpretation of the Taoist doctrine of 'inaction'. "It is not, as some scholars seem to think, 'doing nothing.' It is rather the doctrine of the right opportunity, of acting on the inevitable hour, of striking the timely note that passes into harmony with others and produces a perfect chord." (*Vision of Asia*, Cranmer Byng.) As was said by the Taoist Sage, Chuang Tzu, "The Master came because it was his time to be born; he went, because it was his time to die. For those who accept the phenomenon of birth and death in this sense, lamentation and sorrow have no place." Just as "there is a tide in the affairs of men which, taken at the flood, leads on to fortune," so there is the unique and perfect moment for the commission of each act. He is wise indeed who studies the subtle rhythm of events and learns to act accordingly.

An Action Motiveless

It has been said that the perfect act has no result. This means, of course, that the perfect act is performed so free from personal considerations that in the law of compensation it does not rank as an act performed by that individual. Nor *is* it indeed performed by an individual; rather is it more correct to say, 'there was a performance of the act'. Yet such impersonality can only be achieved by action. We must use action to achieve non-action, purpose to arrive at purposelessness. This may be done by learning to rest the mind on a central, neutral point between the opposites. This is the *laya* centre of Eastern philosophy, the gate through which the unmanifest passes into and back from the manifest. This is what is meant in the *Sutra of Hui Neng* when the Patriarch says, "If we allow our thoughts, the past, the present and the future ones, to link up in a series, we put ourselves under restraint. On the other hand, if we let our mind attach to nothing at all times and towards all things, we gain emancipation. For this reason we take 'Non-attachment' as our fundamental principle." The advantage of this habit, however imperfectly acquired, is pointed out in instruction of Japanese fencing quoted in Dr D. T. Suzuki's third series of *Essays in Zen Buddhism*: "What is most important is to acquire a certain mental attitude known as 'immovable wisdom'. This wisdom is intuitively acquired after a great deal of practical training. 'Immovable' means the highest degree of mobility with a centre which remains immovable. The mind then reaches the highest point of alacrity ready to direct its attention anywhere it is needed."

Such action springs from will, using the term to denote the highest source of spiritual energy as distinct from personal desire. Will is here the voice of the unconscious, in the sense that Dr Suzuki uses the term (*ibid.*): "The Unconscious evolves silently through our empirical individual consciousnesses, and as it thus works, the latter take it for an ego-soul, free, unconditioned and permanent. But when this concept takes hold of our consciousness, the really free activities of the Unconscious meet obstructions on all sides." To remove the restrictions we must remove the thoughts of self, in order that the creative energy of the Unconscious may flow into action without let or hindrance. It is true that "the same outward result may be produced by the victory of the more violent desire as by the use of the will. While the disinclination to get up can be drowned by a heated struggle in which the imagination pictures in glowing colours the advantage to be gained by rising immediately, the same result can be brought about by deleting all pictures, by acting at once and not stopping to think. . . . In the first case the lock is as it were forced, in the other the mechanism is placed in perfect alignment and the key turns noiselessly." (*Yoga and Western Psychology*, Coster.)

Action which springs from will is instantaneous, and knows no intervention of emotion or thought. Describing the secret of Japanese painting, Dr Suzuki says: "The brush must run over the paper swiftly, boldly, fully and irrevocably just like the work of creation when the universe came into being. As soon as a word comes from the mouth of the creator, it must be executed. Delay may mean alteration, which is frustration, or the will has been checked in its forward movement, it halts, it hesitates, it reflects, it reasons, and finally it changes its course—this faltering and wavering interferes with the freedom of the artistic mind." It equally interferes with the freedom of our spiritual activity.

From will to act there must be perfect alignment of energy, a flash of force from highest to lowest unhindered by the intervention of the personality. As Cranmer Byng says in the *Vision of Asia*, "Knowledge and experience are wise counsellors. But the time comes when we must set aside the counsels of deliberation, and act only through the urge from within. Here is the parting of the ways when the false self developed by accretion from without is dissolved, and the true self of divine growth and spiritual adventure takes its place." In such action there is the minimum waste of energy. Thought and emotion use up force, and the manifold desires which pull us hither and thither burn up an immense amount of energy. To act from the inmost centre conserves our vital forces, thus leaving more available for the service of mankind.

If all these arguments are sound, and experience will prove them so, then every passing moment is as important as it is unique. It follows that to move through life with one's mental eyes upon a far horizon is to be in danger of failing in the duty at one's feet. Nor does this imply a concentration upon passing trivialities, for to the wise man there is nothing large and nothing small. This is why in all Zen monasteries the students are made to work in the fields in the intervals of *za-zen*, that is, seated meditation, and in numerous cases they achieve in the fields that spiritual insight called *satori* which they failed to find in the meditation hall. After all, to concentrate one's every faculty upon some physical act itself destroys personality. As a student wrote: "If one is trying to do something really well one becomes, first of all interested in it, and later absorbed in it, which means that one forgets oneself in concentrating on what one is doing. But when one forgets oneself, oneself ceases to exist, since oneself is the only thing which causes oneself to exist." In brief, impersonal action lifts one out of the personality into the realm of 'action purposeless'.

Yet do not be misled into thinking that the doctrine of the act is no more than the due performance of the next task to be done. This, it is true, is the superficial meaning of the Chinese story of the street cleaner. "I asked a poor street cleaner: 'What is the most important work in the Universe?' Looking up, he replied: 'Why, cleaning this street.' " There is a far deeper meaning here. Return once more to the diagram already visualised, and remember that action is Spirit immediately manifest. Now visualise the sequence of events, and remember that they only manifest as sequence owing to our limited consciousness. What follows? Surely that were one single act to be performed quite perfectly we should have risen above the personal, with its limitations of time and place and consequence; in other words, we should have snapped the chain.

CHAPTER ELEVEN

The Jhanas

HAVING APPRECIATED the importance of action as a mode of enlightenment, and thus reduced the risk of being lost in a cloud of abstract doctrine, the student will be ready for a series of exercises which raise the level of consciousness to heights hitherto undreamed of. These different levels of consciousness are found in many languages and many forms. Even the number differs, but one may glean from the Pali Canon a definite series of eight *jhanas*, four lower and four higher, which correlate with the equivalents in Mahayana Buddhism. *Jhana*, the Pali form of the Sanskrit *Dhyana*, passed into China as *Ch'an* and thence to Japan as *Zen*; it is therefore not surprising to find these exercises used alike in Northern and Southern Buddhism, though not always in the same way.

The English language has no equivalent for *jhana*. "Rapture" and "ecstasy" are commonly used, but both connote to Western minds an emotional rather than a truly spiritual experience, while Mrs Rhys Davids' "musing" falls far short of a state which is much too dynamic for such a negative and feeble word. It is better to seek for no equivalent, but to regard the *jhanas* as progressive expansions of consciousness in which the fetters of thought itself, as well as our false ideas on life and matter are dispersed by the rays of enlightenment.

The first *Jhana* is described by the Bhikkhu Silacara as "a state of mind from which for the time being is banished all desire for the pleasurable and delightful, all craving for anything unwholesome, anything making for bondage to the things of sense. In this state, however, there is retained the faculty of taking up a subject of reflection and of dwelling upon it, turning it over and considering it at length; in a word, the ordinary processes of intellection remain active, their working being accompanied by a feeling of pleasure at this temporary release from the thraldom of attachment to objects of sense-delight."

In the second *Jhana* "the mind gradually grows more still, earth and its preoccupations become remote and take on a strange unreality. Sometimes there may even be the sensation of the aspirant's body being suspended in space, with abysses of stars above and below, remote from the haunts of men. The mind, still selfconscious, grows sure of itself, and progresses with a sure step. Concentration is intense, and great joy and peace accompany it." (*Spiritual Exercises*, Tillyard.) It would seem that the mind here approaches the stillness of a mountain pool, unruffled by the conflicting winds of desire. The feeling of impersonal bliss is intensified.

In the third *Jhana*, to quote once more from the Bhikkhu Silacara, "the last shred of delight in the pleasures of sense, even of the most rarified, sublimated description, is transcended, and there is experienced a tranquil all-satisfying happiness, unshadowed by the least disturbance due to any anticipation of happiness to come. This last, technically called *piti*, entirely disappears, and there supervenes a clear, unruffled, perfectly conscious bliss, the bliss of being done with all 'that unrest which men miscall delight'. " Here the sense of self as the subject of this experience is still further diminished, and the meditator no longer feels "It is I who feel this ecstasy, I who am becoming free."

In the fourth, and last of the lower or *rupa jhanas*, the consciousness of the opposites is definitely transcended, and there remains no feeling at all of weal or woe. Described in the Suttas, as 'an utter purity of mindfulness', no further words can usefully describe a state in which the doctrines already expounded in these pages have been so perfectly assimilated, and have produced such immeasurable strength of wisdom poised in inner quietude.

The 'Formless' Jhanas

The dividing line between the *rupa* and *arupa jhanas* is no more precise than that between lower and higher meditation, but the *a-rupa* (without form) *jhanas* aim at a deliberate and progressive expansion of consciousness which is made possible by the purifying process of the lower four. As the higher *jhanas* are states of consciousness which must be experienced to be understood, it would be useless to attempt to describe them in detail here, but the following notes may serve to indicate their essential nature.

The first of the *arupa jhanas* consists in the dying out of all awareness of form, all the discrimination, that is to say, which arises in the mind from comparison between various forms and appearances. By slowly dissolving away the complex forms of 'the 10,000 things' the meditator reaches a condition of 'unbounded space', from which this *jhana* derives its popular name. This process involves a severance of all connection between the senses and the things perceived by sense, a condition in which the world around completely ceases to exist and with it all consciousness of the pairs of opposites. The student may find it useful to attempt this exercise, even at an early stage. Imagine yourself poised in space with the endless forms of life about you reaching outwards to infinity. Dissolve these forms, as boiling water would dissolve a bowl of countless crystals of ice, and there will only remain a sense of infinite space, filled utterly with infinite Life unfettered by outward forms. From such a tremendous dissolution of forms one only will be left—in the centre. Try to dissolve this too, if only for a fleeting second, and know the freedom which comes when the sense of self is dead.

In the second *arupa jhana* the consciousness of boundless space gives way to an infinite comprehension of all knowledge. The feeling is that of an infinite ability to know whatever you want to know, a sense of expansive understanding in which you have but to focus consciousness in any direction to understand it utterly.

The third condition is a state of nothingness, in the sense of no-thing-ness. The consciousness lets go of every concept, even those of boundless space and infinite knowledge, and enters a sphere where no-thing at all exists, not even the perception of nothingness. This utter elimination of all *self*-consciousness is clearly beyond the range of all description, for here the knower and the known are merged in unity.

Still less will words avail for a description of the fourth and last of the formless *jhanas*, for here the most refined of the pairs of opposites are transcended, even that between the all and nothingness, the All and the Void. Here, in a sphere of neither perception nor non-perception, is the limit of all *karmic* action, the state of *Samadhi* which is the final stage of the Noble Eightfold Path.

Such, briefly, are the lower and higher *jhanas* as described in the Scriptures of the Southern School. It will be seen that they range from a state of calm meditation, in which the clamour of the senses is for the moment stilled, to a condition of consciousness which the average mind can scarcely imagine, much less attain. A genuine student should constantly abide in the first of the *rupa*, or lower *jhanas* during meditation, while not a few will find themselves in the second. The third, however, is beyond all but the most exceptional Western minds, save as a very rare and momentary experience, but consistent effort will bring nearer the time when these occasional glimpses are more permanently sustained. The remaining steps will for most of us be trodden in lives to come. Yet once more use the analogy of the spiral, for it illustrates the way in which even these higher stages may be dimly understood, and even to some extent practised by the humblest student, though their final meaning must await more perfect development.

Meditation with and without Seed

The lower and higher groups of *jhanas* correspond to some extent with meditation with and without 'seed'. In the meditation with seed the mind uses a definite object even though it be but an abstract ideal, as the focus of consciousness; in the meditation without seed there is no such focus point, either objective or subjective, and it is therefore, perhaps, more accurate to include such experience under the heading of Contemplation. In meditation with seed, even though the meditator succeeds in stilling the waves of thought and feeling, thus making of his mind a mirror in which true wisdom may be seen, yet these suppressed ideas and feelings remain as tendencies which will reappear in the mind when the intensity of consciousness is removed. These are the 'seeds of habit-energy' referred to in the *Lankavatara Sutra,* described as seeds in that they will reproduce themselves in the mind until such time as they are forever destroyed. In the higher realms of consciousness these former objects of attention lose their power to germinate, and hence to entangle consciousness in the realm of form. The student must therefore sooner or later learn to drop all seed, however tenuous in form, for only so will the mind arrive at the 'vacuum of self-perception' which precedes enlightenment.

The Pause in the Silence.

The student who has raised his consciousness above the limitations of the thinking mind, who has freed himself, at least in meditation, from the grosser forms of self-illusion, and who has attained some measure of control over the faculty of enlightenment must now prepare himself for a further spiritual adventure, contemplation. But between meditation and contemplation there lies a state of consciousness not easily described. It comes at the moment when the seed is dropped, yet before consciousness is attuned to contemplation without seed. It is an emptiness which is at the same time positive, a fierce, dynamic reaching up of consciousness which, having achieved its utmost heights, waits "poised in pure expectancy". Mrs Besant says in *An Introduction to Yoga*, "It is the emptiness of alert expectation, not the emptiness of impending sleep. If your mind be not in that condition, its mere emptiness is dangerous. It leads to mediumship, to possession, to obsession. You can wisely aim at emptiness only when you have so disciplined the mind that it can hold for a considerable time to a single point and remain alert when that point is dropped."

This 'centre in the midst of conditions,' as it is described in *The Secret of the Golden Flower*, is at once the crown of all previous effort and the prelude to greater victories to come. It is a hovering stillness in the silence of a seeming void, a Void which will only be filled when subject and object, the knower, knowing and the known are merged in unity.

But before considering the nature of Contemplation it will be useful to examine the aims and methods of Zen meditation.

CHAPTER TWELVE

Zen Meditation

ZEN IS unique. It therefore defies classification and makes description all but impossible. Reference to the works of the late Dr D. T. Suzuki will tell the student as much as may be known of the history, aim and special methods of Zen, but "the rest is silence—and a finger pointing the way".

The word is a corruption of the Chinese *Ch'an*, which comes from the Sanskrit word *Dhyana*, the Pali equivalent of which is *Jhana*, already familiar to students of this manual. Zen and the *jhanas*, however, have this difference, that the latter are stages of consciousness achieved in definite succession, while Zen is known as the Sudden School. To the extent that Zen is a method it is that of a vigorous advance up the mountain-side without recourse to the well-worn but far longer paths which ultimately reach the same enlightenment. Yet consequences spring from causes, and the achievements of Zen meditation are no less the outcome of lengthy self-development for the fact that they appear with startling suddenness. Nevertheless, while other methods of self-liberation favour a slow, unceasing process of development, Zen leaps upward to the sun.

The dominating factor in the Buddha's life was his Enlightenment. It follows that all Scriptures, doctrines, services, modes of living and methods of meditation must be judged by the sole criterion—Do they or do they not produce Enlightenment? Herein lies the secret of Zen, of its maddening paradoxes and scorn of the conventional, of its fierce impatience with all formulated views and doctrines, and the curious and sometimes violent methods used by masters to assist their pupils to break free. What, then, are the teachings of Zen? The following is an oft-quoted summary:—

"A special transmission outside the Scriptures.
No dependence upon words and letters;
Direct pointing to the soul of man;
Seeing into one's own nature."

In the first proposition lies a secret beyond the scope of this enquiry. A truth explained is a truth no longer true. Words limit, distort, confuse. They are the necessary currency of intellectual thought, but Zen is beyond the intellect. Thereafter reason ceases to hold sway, and the only means of communication is paradox and symbol, and the silent communion of enlightened minds. The highest truths can never be contained in Scriptures; they are handed down through the centuries from teacher to pupil, the former giving to the latter only so much as he is able usefully and safely to receive. Zen masters claim that the Buddha's inmost teaching has been handed down by this imperishable means, this 'special transmission outside the Scriptures' being the very heart of Zen. It follows that no rational method of teaching will suffice to hand on the secret of enlightenment. The master strives to arouse in his pupil a realisation of his own essential nature, and all communication must therefore pass between the intuitive levels of their two minds, without recourse to the distorting mechanism of rational and therefore rationalising thought. Hence the irrational methods of instruction, in which the most absurd, apparently irrelevant, and often, violent phrase or gesture is justified so long as the pupil is thereby freed to the least extent from his own entanglements.

The last three phrases of the foregoing summary will become clearer as this brief exposition proceeds. They are based on the fact that all manifestation is, in the ultimate analysis, illusion, the Essence of life being *tathata*, Suchness, a Fullness which is at the same time a Void. But each minutest form of life is the Universe in miniature, and in attaining Enlightenment each living thing obeys the command: "Become what you are", that is to say, "Look inward—thou *art* Buddha." As is said in the *Sutra of Hui Neng*, " You should know that so far as Buddha-nature is concerned, there is no difference between an enlightened man and an ignorant one. What makes the difference is that one realises it and the other does not."

But the most desperate endeavour to escape from the limitations of form is doomed to failure in a world of form, and in the course of centuries certain ways have been evolved by Zen instructors for handing on their sacred heritage. Not that any Zen master has ever allowed his sole ideal to be dimmed by the intervention of any rigid method or technique. For him there is one purpose in all effort, Enlightenment, and even the most noble ideas and sentiments must bow the knee to this central purpose, or be destroyed. Only such a ruthless integrity of purpose, such a piercing singleness of heart can explain the earnest advice of the master Rinzai: "Inwardly or outwardly, if you encounter any obstacles, kill them right away. If you encounter the Buddha, kill him; if you encounter the Patriarch, kill him; . . . kill them all without hesitation, for this is the only way to deliverance. Do not get yourselves entangled in any object, but stand above, pass on, and be free." Once again one is reminded of the advice in *The Voice of the Silence*: "The Mind is the great Slayer of the Real. Let the Disciple slay the Slayer."

The intensely practical and dynamic nature of Zen explains its lasting effect on the culture, philosophy and social structure of far Eastern nations. It may be this direct simplicity which appeals so much to Westerners, or it may be that the Western mind finds relief from the tyranny of formal thought in a system which so clearly transcends it. Other religions and philosophies seek to build up character, to add new qualities to the spiritual stature of man. Buddhism alone denies the very existence of the individual, the Southern School by a process of negation of each ingredient of the personality, Zen by advising every student to remove or drop each quality or attribute until there is nothing left save his 'original face', that is, his essential nature, which is Buddhahood.

Zen Technique.

Zen meditation may be considered under four headings, namely, its continuity, and the nature of *za-zen*, the *koan* and *mondo*, and *satori*.

1. Meditation must be continuous. As already pointed out in this manual, the most concentrated meditation will have poor results unless the effort be continuous. At the

same time Japanese Zen has achieved a happy compromise between the claims of the 'householder life' and that of the recluse, for whereas it is obvious that one cannot fully concentrate on a *koan* while doing a day's work in an office or factory, yet there are far more persons who wish to obtain the benefits conferred by Zen meditation and discipline than can arrange to abandon all wordly ties and permanently enter a monastery. Most Zen monasteries, accordingly, contain at any given time not only permanent residents, but others who have entered for a specified period, ranging from several months to a mere week-end. During this period, however short, the visitors and permanent residents share the same discipline, outdoor work and hours of meditation. Such a practice, and it is on the increase in Japan, will probably prove the Western answer to a growing need, some place outside the town where one may retire for a definite period for meditation and self-discipline before returning, refreshed and purified in mind and body, to the duties of daily life. At the same time the habits of mind engendered by the regular periods of deep meditation will prevail in the midst of worldliness, and thus bring nearer the day when meditation is in truth continuous.

2. *Za-Zen*, literally, Zen-sitting, is the name given to the sedentary aspect of Zen meditation, as distinct from the constant attitude of mind which is ultimately acquired. In all Zen monasteries the monks sit together in the Meditation Hall, each upright on his own cushion, and meditate on the subject given them separately by the Roshi, the Zen master. There are definite intervals for rest and exercise, and each monk periodically visits the

master to report his progress, if any, and perhaps to receive a new *koan*. In these interviews words are used but sparingly, for the master can perceive by the merest glance or gesture whether the pupil has grasped the meaning of the *koan* given him.

No understanding of *za-zen*, however, is complete without appreciating that it forms but part of the daily round. The motto of Zen monasteries is "No work; no eating," a direct challenge to those monastic orders whose members live on charity. Zen masters have always proclaimed the sanctity of manual labour, and strive to make each monastery self-supporting. Such insistence on manual work as part of the day's routine keeps the body as fit as the mind, prevents laziness and idle introspection, and keeps alive the ideal of applying at once the principles of truth obtained in meditation. As Dr Suzuki points out, "If Zen did not put faith in acting its ideas, the institution would have long before this sunk into a mere somniferous and trace-inducing system, so that all the treasure thoughtfully hoarded by the masters in China and Japan would have been cast away. . . . The fact is that if there is one thing that is most emphatically insisted upon by the Zen masters as the practical expression of their faith, it is serving others, doing work for others, not ostentatiously indeed but secretly, without making others know of it." (*Essays in Zen Buddhism*)

The Koan and Mondo.

3. The *koan* and *mondo*. Just as Zen is unique in the world of Buddhism, so is the *koan* unique in Zen. Its nature is best understood by considering its origin. When

a Message is newly given, its hearers are vitalised by the dynamic qualities of the Message itself. As the years and centuries go by, a process of contraction and hardening sets in, and succeeding masters of the Message find difficulty in keeping its dynamic qualities alive. Concept begins to replace direct experience; the life is enmeshed in the gathering toils of form. Hence the *koan* as a means of handing on the reality of that direct experience which is alone enlightenment. "What the *koan* proposes to do is to develop artificially or systematically in the consciousness of the Zen followers what the early masters produced in themselves spontaneously. It also aspires to develop this Zen experience in a greater number of minds than the master could otherwise hope for. To my mind it was the technique of the *koan* exercise that saved Zen as a unique heritage for Far Eastern-culture. (*ibid*)"

A *koan* is a word, phrase or saying which defies intellectual analysis and thereby enables the user to burst the fetters of conceptual thought. It is the product of experience and of experience alone. "All *koans* are the utterances of *satori* with no intellectual mediations; hence their uncouthness and incomprehensibility. The Zen master has no deliberate scheme on his part to make his statements of *satori* uncouth or logically unpalatable; the statements come forth from his inner being, as flowers burst out in spring-time, or as the sun sheds its rays. Therefore, to understand them we have to be like flowers or like the sun; we must enter into their inner being." (*ibid*). In order, therefore, to understand a *koan* we must reproduce in ourselves the same conditions of consciousness as gave it birth. Here are a few examples:—

Two hands when clapped make a certain sound. What is the sound of one hand clapping?

What was your original face before your parents were born?

All things may be reduced to the One. To what is the One reduced?

Is there Buddha-nature in a dog? Joshu answered "Mu" (literally "No" or "None").

Empty-handed I go and lo! the spade's in my hand.

When I pass over the bridge the water flows not, but the bridge flows.

A cow passed through a window. Its head, body and legs passed easily; only its tail could not pass through. Why not?

Why are such *koans* given? The idea is to reproduce in the mind of the pupil the state of consciousness of which these statements are the expression. At their own level they are not problems at all, and it follows that by raising one's consciousness high enough the problem is thereby solved. The *koan* is thus a means and not an end. It is a tool to be used and discarded, a raft to be used in crossing the stream, then left behind. A *koan* has no 'answer' which can be written down, for such would at once degrade it to the level of the intellect. The *koan* is a sign-post or clue to a state of consciousness in which alone the answers abides. Its purpose is therefore to work up an ever-increasing pressure of 'searching and contriving,' which leads in time to a state of intellectual bankruptcy. Then, when the process of thought can go no further, the student must summon the courage to abandon all, 'leap over the precipice,' and find in the death of thought the birth of Enlightenment.

The process of 'letting go' is essential. So long as the student clings to the intellect, the world of enlightenment will remain closed. Each spark of life must sooner or later free itself from the complex structure of thought within which a higher faculty has been slowly brought to birth. The caterpillar weaves a cocoon in which to achieve its fundamental change, but before it can enter the world of light it must needs abandon the chrysalis. Yet there is no question of weak passivity in this letting go. Zen meditation calls for an 'iron determination and indomitable will,' yet this dynamic intensity of purpose is quite compatible with an inner quietude. In the words of *The Voice of the Silence*, "both action and inaction may find room in thee; thy body agitated, thy mind tranquil, thy soul as limpid as mountain lake".

The fact that this effort is so intense and so continuous involves an element of danger. The change from intellectual to intuitive processes throws great strain upon the brain. As H. P. Blavatsky once said, "The brain is the instrument of waking consciousness, and every conscious mental picture formed means change and destruction of the atoms of the brain. Ordinary intellectual activity moves on well-beaten paths in the brain, and does not compel sudden adjustments and destructions in its substance. But this new kind of mental effort calls for something very different, the carving out of new 'brain paths' the ranking in different order of the little brain lives. If forced injudiciously it may do serious physical harm to the brain."

The Use of a Koan

The process is thus threefold. First, the mind is concentrated on the *koan* until the intellect is utterly exhausted and, as it were, burnt out. Then comes a pause, a suspension of all function in a nameless emptiness, a severance of every tie, a letting go. Then only comes the 'answer,' a flash of understanding which, according as it is partial or complete, shatters or merely loosens the fetters of conceptual thought. Few achieve this level without an effort which exhausts the personality. As a Zen master said, "Unless you have been thoroughly drenched in perspiration you cannot expect to see a palace of pearls on a blade of grass."

No barriers can stand against this tremendous spirit of enquiry; they do but strengthen the indomitable will to know. "The fact that all great masters have been willing to give themselves up, body and soul, to the mastery of Zen proves the greatness of their faith in ultimate reality, and also the strength of their spirit of enquiry, known as 'seeking and contriving,' which never suspends its activity until it attains its end." (Suzuki. *Essays in Zen Buddhism*).

The *mondo* is a rapid exchange of question and answer between master and pupil. In many cases, as in Joshu's "Mu," the answer is itself a *koan*; in other cases the question and answer must be considered as a whole.

Here are some examples:—

A monk asked Joshu, "What is the one ultimate word of truth?" Joshu replied: "Yes".

Another monk asked another master the same question, The reply was: "You make it two."

"What is my self?" "What would you do with a self?"

"What is Tao?" "Usual life is very Tao." "How can we accord with it?" "If you try to accord with it you will get away from it."

"All things are such as they are from the beginning; what is that which is beyond existence?" "Your statement is quite plain. Why ask me?"

Note how the answer throws the question back into the questioner's mind, where alone a solution may be found. Note, too, how homely and practical the answers seem when compared with those which a lesser mind might give. Would the seeker after the 'ultimate word of truth' be the more enlightened by an answer couched in abstract principles? Such answers do but echo those of the Buddha as recorded in the Pali Scriptures, where again and again we find that he refused to answer in words a question which could only be answered by inward experience. Zen answers are but one remove from the Buddha's 'noble silence.' The *mondo* cuts off speculation, stills the intellect and calls on a higher faculty. Provided this is the *result* of the answer, its form is immaterial. One knows so well the mind which asks 'about it and about,' and cannot see that the answer will still be *about* the question, and not a means to enlightenment. Hence the resort by certain masters to astonishing methods of tearing open this cocoon of argument. If a blow is likely to crack this shell of intellectual doubt it is promptly given, and a shout or grimace may have the same effect.

Zen masters are equally famous for their unconven-

tional sermons. Here, for example, is one in its entirety.
"If you have a staff I will give you one; if you have not
I will take it away from you." (One is tempted to quote
as a remarkable parallel the New Testament saying that
to him that hath shall be given, and from him that hath
not shall be taken away even that which he hath.) Other
great masters have preached to their followers more briefly
still. More than one has entered the pulpit and made but
a single gesture, such as opening wide his arms, yet this
was enough for those whose 'eye of truth' was all but
opened, and *satori* came.

Attempts have been made to classify the various types
of *koan* and *mondo*, and Dr Suzuki has done so at some
length. Yet all have a common aim, the attainment of
enlightenment by direct action. The 'contrivances' may
differ, but the end is the same.

Satori.

Satori is the *raison d'être* of Zen, and the whole purpose
of the *koan* exercise. Dr Suzuki defines it as "an intuitive
looking into the nature of things in contradistinction to
the analytical or logical understanding of it". But the
intuition is above duality. "The general feeling which
characterizes all our functions of consciousness is that of
restriction and dependence, because consciousness itself
is the outcome of two forces conditioning or restricting
each other. Satori, on the contrary, essentially consists in
doing away with the opposition of two terms in whatever
sense." Hence the tremendous statement of Zen masters
that manifestation, the Wheel of Samsara, is itself Reality,
in that Samsara and Nirvana are ultimately One. To

describe such an experience one can only use analogy. It seems that, using the *koan* as a focus point of will, the intellect is driven to its utmost limits and then, like the leap of an electric spark between two terminals, thinker and thought are fused in unity. Here is the realm of the higher third, the unifying point of view above all opposites. It is only attained by tremendous effort, the 'emptiness' of which it is the outcome being the very antithesis of mere vacuity. Rather it is the result of the 'spiritual poverty' attained in *zazen*. "Give up thy life if thou wouldst live," says *The Voice of the Silence*, and the same advice was given by the master Kyogen:—

"My last year's poverty was not poverty enough.
My poverty this year is poverty indeed.
In my poverty last year there was room for a
gimlet's point,
But this year even the gimlet is gone."

Yet the fulness of *satori*, which ensues upon the utter emptiness which is the achievement of *zazen*, is a fulness without limit, a fusion of the spark with the Flame, of the individual with the Universal Consciousness.

Satori is a momentary alignment of all one's vehicles with the Universal Mind which uses them, an irradiation of one's whole being with the warmth and fire of enlightenment. In terms of psychology it is a fusion of the diverse parts of one's being, the unconscious, conscious and superconscious, in conscious unity. As Dr Suzuki says, "The will is the man himself and Zen appeals to it." By the *koan* exercises "the more superficial activity of the mind is set at rest so that its more central and profounder parts which are generally deeply buried can be brought out and exercised to perform their native functions." One of the 'native functions' of these deeply buried faculties is that of direct action, action which springs from the will without the mediation of any intellectual process; hence the right use of action as a contrivance for freeing the will from the inhibitions which lie hidden in the unconscious mind. A monk complained to the master Bokuji and said, "We have to dress and eat every day. How can we escape from all that?" The master replied, "We dress; we eat." "I do not understand you," said the questioner." "Then put your dress on and eat your food," was the reply.

In the light of these observations the purpose of *koans* may become more clear. Thus many of them, for example Joshu's "*Mu*," are designed to raise the consciousness above duality by denying every predicate, positive or negative, concerning the object under review, thus pointing the way to direct experience. To assert that the Buddha is in a dog or to assert that he is not are both inadequate assertions, for both admit a distinction between two things which are not two but one. Again, speaking of 'the sound of one hand,' Professor Pratt says: "It is not a sound nor a sensation, but a state of mind. A sound is made by something which is in relation to something else—as the first sound made by the two hands. In the Absolute there are no relations and distinctions. The attempt to hear the sound of one hand is merely one of the many ways of bringing the pupil to this realization" (*Pilgrimage of Buddhism*). Not that any words can 'explain' a *koan*, but these two examples may help to make clear the state of consciousness which they are designed to achieve.

There are many degrees of *satori*, ranging from a flash of intuitive understanding to full Enlightenment. Presumably the different grades of *koan* collate with the grades or levels of *satori*. As ever harder *koans* are solved, the unconscious more and more invades the conscious mind, and the personal self is jettisoned in favour of an ever widening point of view. As the *koan* gets more difficult, and deeper understanding fills the mind, the claims of humanity begin to predominate until the individual consciousness is merged in the Universal Mind. Then only is the Unconscious of the individual and the Unconscious of the Universe made one, and self, bereft of any abiding place, dissolves in nothingness.

Beware of false *satori*, for the toils of illusion grow more subtle as we tread the Path, and much that is claimed as a wondrous spiritual experience is only phantasy. The stranger who enters a new land may be easily deceived by appearances, and there is no end to the self-induced illusion which the seeking mind will manufacture to achieve its end. Yet the tree is known by its fruit, and the touchstone of *satori* is its effect on character.

The Effects of Satori

In the opinion of Dr Suzuki, "the opening of *satori* is the remaking of life itself." It is a spiritual rebirth, a return to the child state in the sense of an utter honesty of thought and speech, and a simple directness of action. These are the indications of *satori*, together with a width of vision and an inner quietude which come from genuine experience. The effects on character will naturally reflect the degree of *satori* attained. A mere glimpse of the higher world may leave but a memory; the attainment of Samadhi is the death of self. Between these two extremes lies every degree of improvement, yet there is a definite moment when the cumulative effect of *koan* exercises lifts the spiritual centre of gravity out of the world of self-ambition into the world of selflessness. This is the 'rebirth' of the ancient Mysteries, a 'crossing the stream' to the shores of another world. Yet this is not the end, the final goal. "Veil after veil must lift—but there must be veil upon veil behind." Such further travel has no practical concern for most of us, yet we may tread without delay in the footsteps of those who claim to be treading directly in the footsteps of the All-Enlightened One.

This, then, is the secret of Zen, that it uses the mind to surmount the mind, and with or without the aid of a graduated series of *koans* bursts through into a state of consciousness which lies above duality, and hence beyond the sway of all comparisons and distinctions. The sole concern of Zen is to attain enlightenment, and all which stands in the way is made to serve this end or be flung aside. For dynamic singleness of purpose it has no equal, and its technique is designed to serve this end. No words are wasted on the pupil. The goal is pointed out to him, the obstacles made clear; the rest is silence—and a finger pointing the Way.

Part Four

CONTEMPLATION

CHAPTER THIRTEEN

Contemplation

IF IT is difficult to put into words the technique and experiences of Higher Meditation, it is wellnigh impossible to write of a higher process still. At such a level to assert is to limit, to describe is to degrade. As is said in the *Lankavatara Sutra*: "If you assert that there is such a thing as Noble Wisdom, it no longer holds good, because anything of which something is asserted thereby partakes of the nature of being and is thus characterised with the quality of birth. The very assertion: 'All things are unborn,' destroys the truthfulness of it. The same is true of the statements: 'All things are empty,' and 'All things have no self-nature'—both are untenable when put in the form of assertions." Yet, remembering the analogy of the spiral, the student may glimpse a faint reflection of a state of consciousness which is above description because above all predicates.

Contemplation is an utterly impersonal awareness of the essence of the thing observed. Its technique, if one may use such a word in this connection, consists in achieving the utmost one-pointedness of thought upon a given subject and then raising one's conception of the subject at the same time as one's consciousness. In concentration, the concrete mind is fixed, let us say, on something round. In meditation, the consciousness is raised to the abstract mind and the subject to its highest form, that is to say, to the abstract conception of roundness which its form enshrines. In contemplation, the consciousness becomes completely impersonal, a focus of attention upon a subject which is now perceived in its inmost essence bereft of any form. The nature of the subject is immaterial, for the contemplator KNOWS that its inmost essence and his own are aspects of the same Universal Essence of Pure Mind. Whatever the ideal may be, the contemplator sees it for the first time as it is. Mystics speak of this condition as being face to face with the Beloved, of gazing upon their own Divinity; others describe it as being poised in a world of infinite quietude before a subject which is no longer limited by form, but stands as a symbol of the Not-Self which is for the first time seen to be the ultimate SELF made manifest.

In this condition the inmost Self of the contemplator is free to function on its own plane, having severed the bonds which fettered it to form. Whereas in concentration the intellect was taught to function without hindrance from the senses, and in meditation the intuitive mind was taught to rise superior to the intellect, in contemplation the whole machinery of the mind is made quiescent, and the naked spark perceives the Flame unveiled.

Yet just as a man at the top of a light-house may speak direct to the ground without his message being relayed at the intervening storeys, so the brain in contemplation sees in flashes of inspired perception the realm of Spirit, where the contemplator stands at the threshold of his own Enlightenment. All intervening processes of thought are set aside; "the insight of the wise who move about in the realm of imagelessness and its solitude is pure. That is, for the wise all 'things' are wiped away and even the state of imagelessness ceases to exist." (*ibid.*) The channel

214

between spirit and matter, between spiritual understanding and its lowest instrument, the brain, is for the moment unobstructed, and within the framework of his limitations the student for the moment KNOWS.

At such a level every man-made form is valueless. All religions are transcended, and all distinctions between *methods* of attainment null and void. It is only at such an exalted level, when the contemplator "penetrates beyond all images, however lovely, however significant, to that ineffable awareness which the mystics call 'Naked Contemplation'—since it is stripped of all the clothing with which reason and imagination drape and disguise both our devils and our gods—that the hunger and thirst of the heart is satisfied, and we receive indeed an assurance of ultimate Reality. This assurance is not the cool conclusion of a successful argument. It is rather the seizing at last of Something which we have ever felt near us and enticing us; the unspeakably simple because completely inclusive solution of all puzzles of life." (*Practical Mysticism*. Underhill.)

In terms of mysticism, the contemplating consciousness perceives the Universal in each particular, the All in every part. Without losing self-consciousness, in the sense of an awareness of individuality, the contemplator perceives his identity with all the Universe, and knows that knowledge in the brain. At first this understanding comes in flashes of *satori*, as followers of Zen would say. Later the vision becomes more permanent, with corresponding effects upon the spiritual grandeur of the awakening mind. At this exalted level he solves at last the paradox of self. There is no longer any higher self, nor lower; only two facets of a perfect whole. He sees his inmost essence in the Essence of Pure Mind, yet in the world of illusion sees the same Self immanent in all. This dual process enables him to unite in one the claims of spirit and matter, those of the inner worlds and the world of every day. Freed from the tyranny of sense-reaction, he works in the world with a deeper insight to its needs, yet never loses contact with that Essence of Mind which is alone Reality.

When contemplation has become at last a permanent condition, there remains but one link binding him to the Wheel of Suffering—his will to serve humanity. Before such mighty beings lies the threshold of supreme Enlightenment. Some enter; some return. The latter are they who, having reached the Goal, come back to point the Way to those who sit in darkness, for they know that all who contemplate illusion will ultimately turn about and face enlightenment. Then will they too achieve this 'centre of a circle centreless', and point the Way in turn to those less fortunate. Naught hinders any man in such achievement—save self, and the toils of circumstance self-forged and self-imposed. Then strive for the realm of Contemplation, for it has been said: "In Contemplation we step out of existence into Being, out of the confines of time and space into the Eternal Now. Here dwells the Fountain. Take what you will."

CHAPTER FOURTEEN

Conclusion

"THOSE WHO would enter from the outer court, where flowers are offered to the figure of Gotama, into the inner sanctuary, where the heart of the teacher is understood, can only do so by the discipline of meditation." (*Spiritual Exercises*. Tillyard.)

Such are the views of those who compiled this manual. To summarise its contents would be to interpose a mere opinion between the material here presented and the student's mind. There are, however, five matters which need to be strongly emphasised.

Meditation is a positive, dynamic process, a vital self-renewing and not a negative escape from life. As the translator of *The Secret of the Golden Flower* points out: "Much has been taught the modern man in recent years about the hitherto unsuspected elements in his psyche, but the emphasis is all too often on the static side alone, so that he finds himself possessed of little more than an inventory of contents, the nature of which serves to burden him with a sense of weariness rather than to spur him on to master the problems that confront him. Yet it is precisely the need of understanding himself in terms of change and renewal which most grips the imagination of modern man." Morality is equally revitalised. The smug complacency of negative goodness is replaced by a living sense of eternal values, in which the will to do right out-weighs the fear of doing what others may hold to be wrong. Whether one adopts the gentle methods of self-surrender as typified in Taoism, or the strenuous methods of self-conquest found in Yoga, the same war must be waged and the same enemy overcome. Methods may vary with temperament, but the goal is the same for all, the fusion of all aspects of our complex being in a limitless, enlightened whole.

The means must always be subordinated to the end. To stress the importance of method is as foolish as concentration on the finger which points the way. Yet all religions and their scriptures, and all schools of self-development are only methods, and all alike are subject to the laws of form. They are born, they grow up, they grow old, they die. Truth, alone is constant and the way to it, for all methods are only methods of this Way. Zen is supreme in this respect, that it never loses sight of its essential purpose, the attainment of enlightenment. All methods, from a particular exercise to a particular religion, should be used as a craftsman uses different tools to create his masterpiece. He has his favourite tools for a particular purpose, but one and all, when they have served their purpose, are laid away. The sole and only use of any method is to acquire experience, and all discussions, books and lectures are a futile waste of time unless they serve this end.

The motive must be pure and definite, and the wise man sees that it is constantly reviewed. Of all the multifarious reasons why men and women meditate just one is right, the genuine desire to achieve for all mankind as well as for oneself supreme Enlightenment.

No Master will appear to guide the student's footsteps until he has trodden the preliminary stages alone. The

Master M. has made this clear. "It is the common mistake of people that we willingly wrap ourselves and our powers in mystery. . . . The truth is that till the neophyte attains to the condition necessary for that degree of Illumination to which, and for which, he is entitled and fitted, most *if not all* of the secrets are *incommunicable.* The receptivity must be equal to the desire to instruct. The illumination *must come from within.*" (*Mahatma Letters.*) To choose one's *guru* is itself most difficult, and few who lightly register themselves as pupils of the latest 'adept' have any conception of what such a relationship implies. Such blind obedience to a man whose bold pretensions they are unable to examine is a self-entanglement in further fetters, making it yet more difficult to obey the Buddha's exhortation to work out their own salvation with diligence. The hall-mark of the fake is the taking of money, or the making of claims, and no genuine Teacher will permit his followers to worship him. The hall-mark of the genuine Teacher, on the other hand, is a deep and genuine humility, and an all-pervading will to serve mankind.

The Duty to Teach

Finally, remember that our growing knowledge must be shared with others still more ignorant. True, we have no right to force the truth on any man, but we have a duty to see that none shall walk in ignorance for want of our willingness to share with him such knowledge as we have. The Master K.H. speaks of the "prime duty of gaining knowledge and disseminating through all available channels such fragments as mankind in the mass may be ready to assimilate". (*ibid.*) Nor is it of the least value to acquire knowledge for oneself alone. Just as the blood is the common property of every physical cell, so knowledge should revitalise each aspect of the Universal Mind. Be not afraid of casting pearls before swine. It is true that knowledge is power, and to hand it on is to assume the *karma* of its possible misuse, but the elementary principles of which the 'man in the street' has such pathetic need are not so dangerous that we may not share them willingly wherever the genuine desire for knowledge is made plain. Yet none will thank you for this priceless boon. All who have striven to offer truth to humanity have suffered persecution and vile abuse. There was a time when they were stoned to death by the multitude, or burnt at the stake. To-day they are attacked with no less fear-inspired savagery by the forces of so-called science and religion, and by the mass resistance of blind ignorance as brought to focus by the Press. As the Master K.H. wrote of the Brotherhood to Sinnett: "The first and last consideration is whether we can do good to our neighbour, no matter how humble he may be; and we do not permit ourselves to even think of the danger of any contumely, abuse or injustice visited upon ourselves. We are ready to be 'spat upon and crucified' daily—not once —if real good to another can come of it." (*ibid.*) Be ever on the watch, then, to share the fruits of your experience. There is timeless wisdom in *The Voice of the Silence* when it speaks: "Point out the 'Way'—however dimly, and lost among the host—as does the evening star to those who tread their path in darkness. . . . Give light and comfort to the toiling pilgrim, and seek out him who

THE DUTY TO TEACH

knows still less than thou . . . and let him hear the Law."

Thus meditating positively and untiringly, with unselfish motive and eyes that see beyond all method to the chosen end, not seeking a Guru on whom to lay the burden of one's *karmic* hindrances, but ever willing to share with a fellow pilgrim every crust of knowledge gained, the student will ultimately graduate in wisdom, and find himself before the threshold of Supreme Enlightenment—only to find that Enlightenment itself is but a veil, concealing a quite ineffable Beyond.

APPENDIX ONE

Notes on Group Meditation

IT IS axiomatic that the united strength of many is greater than the strength of one, and the system of regular meetings for the study and practice of meditation has much to recommend it. There are those who lack the courage or determination to begin alone, or find that when they do so they become too negative. Again, there is always a gulf between the text-book and actual practice. Practical problems arise which the experience of other members of a group may help to solve, for in a group the joint experience of the trials and errors of actual meditation are at the service of all. Finally, in a well-chosen and well-conducted group there is a sense of genuine brotherhood which is in itself a wonderful experience.

The group may be one of three kinds, scattered, collected or a mixture of both. If the members are scattered geographically, their collective work must consist of common times or subjects of meditation, and a system of correspondence by which the results are collected and placed at the disposal of all. Some groups, however, are partly scattered and partly accessible to a central meeting place. They thus consist of an inner circle of those who meet in the physical body, and a scattered remainder who keep in touch by thought and correspondence. Those less fortunate naturally 'tune in' at the time of the meeting, just as those at the meeting link up in thought with every member wherever situate.

The third type is of two kinds. There are a few groups

in the West which are fortunate enought to have a leader qualified to instruct and guide the members in their search for higher experience. Such teachers are most rare, though of those who imagine themselves so qualified there is no end. Most groups, however, have no member qualified to act as teacher, and it is to this type that the following notes apply:—

The Leader

The leader of the group, in the sense of the person conducting the meetings, should either be the person most obviously suitable or else be changed at intervals. This latter practice will quench any spark of jealousy, and accustom different members to the cares and responsibilities of leadership. Once the leader is elected for a certain period he should demand and receive the utmost loyalty, and insist that any criticism of his leadership be spoken to his face. Only in such an atmosphere of mutual trust, respect and goodwill can useful work be done in a group which is dedicated to spiritual things.

Choice of Members

The choice of members must be made most carefully. Each must be utterly sincere, determined to continue in the face of every difficulty, unselfish to the interests of the group without reference to his own, and unswervingly loyal. Furthermore, the members as a whole must harmonise, for a member, however advanced, who is out of tune with the others will wreck the group activities. The members must be 'as the fingers of one hand,' practising genuine brotherhood the one with the other, and deaf to all gossip of each other's faults and failings.

The Choice of Subject

The subject chosen should be a saying, principle or diagram rather than a collective calling down of higher forces. The latter is, needless to say, a far more powerful use of collective effort, for it builds a thought-form on the inner planes which serves as a channel between the higher and lower levels of consciousness. Rightly formed, controlled and used, such a thought-form can be of enormous service to the group and its environment, but unless carefully controlled by someone with occult knowledge it is better left unformed. What one has built another may use, and there are evil powers as well as good beyond the realm of daily happenings. Even if the leader knows how to control the forces which pour through such a channel it does not follow that each member can assimilate them, and the strength and profound effect of these forces must be experienced to be believed.

Meetings

Meetings should be regular, and at the same time and place. Every member should arrive punctually, letting nothing short of definite illness keep him or her away. On arrival, he should try to leave all worldly thought and worries outside the door. Once seated in the circle, he must remember that he has come to give and not to receive, to learn and not to show how much he knows. All group matters should be settled quite informally. Conventional procedure should be avoided and discussion reduced to a minimum. The meeting should then begin with a collective raising of consciousness above the personality, and a linking up at the highest level possible. Meditation on the chosen subject should be short and intense, ten minutes being quite long enough for beginners. While meditating, each member should strive to sink his own self in that of the group, for this deliberate expansion of consciousness into that of a larger unit is one of the most valuable products of group meditation. It has been said: "The group is the self of the altruist. The great man actually feels towards the group as the little man feels towards himself." The time will come when the 'group' will be all humanity.

Subjects for Meditation

Note: It has been suggested that a list of valuable sayings and phrases would be a useful addition to this manual. The following list has therefore been compiled. It might be indefinitely extended, but the selection here appended will provide material for meditation to suit all needs. The sayings may be used in actual meditation or as the focus of thought during idle moments of the day. No attempt has been made at classification, nor is the source given, even when known.

*　　*　　*

To live to benefit mankind is the first step.

Kill out desire.

Walk on.

Live in the Eternal.

Thou art Buddha.

To meditate is to realise inwardly the imperturbability of the Essence of Mind.

Will is the Lord of Karma.

Deny nothing. Affirm all.

The light is within you. Let the light shine.

Behind will stands desire.

No origin is the highest good.

Draw a line from North to South and there is neither East nor West.

The hill goes up and down.

We behold that which we are.

I am not yet I am.

Forgoing self the Universe grows I.

To love universally is true humility.

It's all right.

There is no death.

I wept into the sea: it did not overflow.

The perfect act has no result.

To the enlightened everywhere is the same.

There is nothing great: there is nothing small.

What comes to me is a return to me of what goes out of me.

The future does not come from before to meet us; it comes streaming up from behind over our heads.

Be humble and you will remain entire.

Man stands in his own shadow and wonders why it is dark.

There is nothing infinite apart from finite things.

There is no poverty save in desire.

There is nothing good nor ill but thinking makes it so.

The cause of death is birth.

In every aspiration dwells the certainty of its own fulfilment.

Become what you are.

If any man be unhappy, let him know that it is by reason of himself alone.

Aim at extreme disinterestedness, and maintain at all times the utmost possible calm.

By concentrating the thoughts one can fly; by concentrating the desires one falls.

To girdle the earth needs but to place one foot before the other—unceasingly.

"Master, what can I do to help the world?"
"What *can* you do?"

There is no such thing as sacrifice; there is only opportunity to serve.

The wise man is to be distinguished from his fellow men by his peculiar independence of external things.

The Teacher can but point the Way.

Better you should be sullied while trying to help those in the mire than that you should stand aloof and remain clean.

The sage, however, does not judge; he tries to understand.

Desire only that which is within you.

We have many duties but only one right, opportunity, and that we earn.

Give up thy life if thou wouldst live.

We are not what we think we are but what we think we are.

The measure of our immortality is the frequency of our immortal acts.

The land that is nowhere, that is the true home.

A man may know he can succeed, and yet fail; but unless he knows he can succeed he never will.

Life is a bridge; pass over it but build no house on it.

Disease is not cured by pronouncing the name of medicine.

There is nothing yonder than cannot be found here.

There is no such thing as adversity.

Foolish are they who turn their backs on the light and argue over the shadow in front.

The truly happy are those who bring their desires into line with their duty.

Love is the fulfiling of the law.

Man walks on two legs.

The heart of the perfect man is a mirror; it reflects all things but holds nothing for itself alone.

Saying "Let me help you out of the water or you will drown," the kindly monkey put the fish safely up a tree.

The dewdrop regarded the sun with envy and said: "I am That." And the sun took it at its word.

One came to the master and said: "How shall I be delivered from the Wheel of birth and death?" And the master said: "Who puts you under restraint?"

Two men looked into a pond. Said the one: "I see a quantity of mud, a shoe and an old tin can." Said the other: "I see all these, but I also see the glorious reflection of the sky."

An aged Brahman came to the Buddha, bearing gifts in either hand. Said the Buddha: "Drop it." The Brahman let fall one of his gifts. Again the order came: "Drop it." The Brahman dropped the other gift.

Again the order came. The Brahman was for the moment at a loss, then smiled, for he had attained enlightenment.

An Indian prince once gave a ring to his jeweller and asked him to engrave in it a sentence which would support him in adversity and restrain him in prosperity. The jeweller engraved therein this sentence: "It will pass."

I have no parents. I make heaven and earth my parents. I have no strength. I make submission my strength. I have neither life nor death. I make the self-existent my life and death. I have no friends. I make my mind my friend. I have no armour. I make right thinking and right-doing my armour. I have no sword. I make the sleep of the mind my sword.

Zen has nothing to say.

Glossary

of Certain Technical Terms
used in this Manual

Note: See also *A Popular Dictionary of Buddhism.* Christmas Humphreys (Arco).

ABSOLUTE, The: Parinirvana, "an Omnipresent, Eternal, Boundless and Immutable Principle on which all speculation is impossible, since it transcends the power of human conception and could only be dwarfed by any human expression or similitude. It is beyond the range and reach of thought." Absolute Truth: the truth about the Absolute, utterly beyond our ken.

ANATTA: The doctrine of non-ego, one of the three characteristics of existence, in which all is *anicca, dukkha, anatta.* That which is called the ego, which says 'I am', is merely an aggregate of *skandhas*, a complex of sensations, ideas, thoughts, emotions and volitions. It is not an eternal, immutable entity behind these, separating him from the One Life, which shines through every form of life from mineral to man.

ANICCA: Impermanence; one of the three characteristics of all existence: *anatta, dukkha, anicca.* The doctrine teaches that everything is subject to the law of cause and effect, is the creation of preceding causes and is in its turn a cause of after effects. There is in existence, therefore, no stable being, but only an everbecoming flux.

ARHAT: The Worthy One. One who has traversed the Eightfold Path to the Goal, eliminated the ten Fetters and the four Defilements which bind to existence, and on the death of the physical body attains Nirvana.

ASCETICISM: As practised for gaining magical powers or propitiating gods essentially selfish. In First Sermon Buddha condemned extreme asceticism as ignoble and useless, and taught Middle Way between self-mortification and allurements of senses. Only asceticism Buddhism permits is abstinence and bodily self-control as aids to mental self-control, practice of virtue and altruism: *i.e.*, renunciation of temporary pleasure for permanent happiness.

AST; NASTI: To be, not to be.

ATMAN. (See Self.)

AVIDYA (Sk.) AVIJJA (P.): Ignorance; lack of enlightenment; the fundamental root of evil, and the ultimate cause of the desire which creates the *dukkha* of existence. Its total elimination, resulting in perfect enlightenment, is the Goal of Buddhist Path. Ignorance is first of the Twelve Nidanas or Links in the Chain of Causation; first because it is the primary cause of existence. It is the last of the Ten Fetters; last because until full enlightenment is attained there still remains some degree of error or ignorance. The final removal of the veil of ignorance reveals supreme Truth—Nirvana.

BHAVANA: Lit. a 'making-to-become'. Self-development by any means, but especially by the method of mind-control, concentration and meditation.

BHIKKHU (P.) BHIKSHU (Sk.): A member of the

Sangha, one who has devoted himself to the task of following the Path by renunciation of the distractions of worldly affairs. (See Sangha.)

BODHISATTA (P.) BODHISATTVA (Sk.): One whose 'being' or 'essence' (*sattva*) is *bodhi*, that is, the wisdom resulting from direct perception of Truth, with the compassion awakened thereby.

In Theravada, an aspirant for Buddha-hood: the Buddha is described in Jataka accounts of his former lives as the *Bodhisatta*.

In Mahayana, the Bodhisattva is the ideal of the Path as contrasted with the Arahat of the Theravada. He is one who, having practised the Ten Paramitas and attained Enlightenment, renounces Nirvana in order to help humanity on its pilgrimage. The Bodhisattvas are often called 'Buddhas of Compassion', as love in action guided by wisdom is their aim.

BUDDHA: A title, not the name of a person; derived from root *budh*, to know, it means one who knows, *i.e.*, has become one with the highest knowledge, Supreme Truth.

BUDDHI: Spiritual Wisdom. Universal Mind mirrored in the heart of man: the source of *bodhi*. The link between Ultimate Reality and the Mind (*Manas*). The sixth principle in the sevenfold constitution of man taught in the esoteric schools of Buddhism.

DANA: The virtue of alms-giving to the poor and needy; also making gifts to a bhikkhu or community of bhikkhus. One of the three 'acts of merit', *dana*, benevolence; *sila*, moral conduct; *bhavana*, meditation. Dana in Buddhism takes the place of sacrificial rites in Hinduism.

DHAMMAPADA: Collection of Verses. Famous Pâli Scripture. Many English translations.

DUKKHA: Often translated as suffering, but signifying rather dis-ease, dis-comfort, dis-satisfaction, ill-being or disharmony with environment. The assertion that life is *dukkha* is one of the Four Noble Truths, being naturally associated with every effort to adapt oneself to that ever-changing environment which is the outcome of the 'will to live'. Complete escape from *dukkha* is possible only by liberation from the round of birth and death.

FIRES, The Three: *Dosa* (anger, ill-will, hatred), *Lobha* (covetousness or greed), *Moha* (mental dullness or stupidity).

FOUR NOBLE TRUTHS, The. These are:

(1) All existence is Suffering (v. Dukkha.) All states of mind which arise from the sense of separateness are states of sorrow or ill.

(2) The Cause of Suffering is selfish craving (*tanha*), desire for separate existence consequent on sense attraction.

(3) The Cessation of Suffering is attained by the elimination of this thirst for separate existence. This is attained by following the Noble Eightfold Path, which is the

(4) Way to the Ceasing of Suffering. "This especially

do I teach," said the Buddha, "Suffering and the ending of Suffering."

This Way is the Noble Eightfold Path.

HINAYANA: Historically, the earliest school of Buddhism. The term is of mild reproach coined by members of the Mahayana (q.v.) to describe this 'small vehicle' as distinct from their own 'great vehicle' (of salvation). Its only surviving sect is the Theravada (q.v.).

KÂMA: desire of the senses, especially sexual desire. The kâma-loka are the worlds of sense desire or purgatorial after-death states. Kâma must not be confused with *karma* (q.v.).

KARMA: Pali *kamma*. Root meaning "action"; derived meaning, "action and the appropriate result of action"; the law of cause and effect. Karma operates on all planes of existence. As applied to the moral sphere it is the Law of Ethical Causation, through the operation of which a man "reaps what he sows," builds his character, makes his destiny, and works out his salvation.

Karma is not limited by time or space, and is not strictly individual; there is group karma, family, national, etc. See *W.B.*, pp. 67 and 90.

The doctrine of re-birth is an essential corollary to that of karma, the individual coming into physical life with a character and into an environment resulting from his actions in the past. His character and destiny are, therefore, popularly (and correctly) called his "karma", and according to his reaction to his present destiny he modifies and builds his future.

LANOO: a disciple.

MAHAYANA: The School of the "Great Vehicle" of Salvation, also called the "Northern School". Geographically it includes Tibet and Mongolia (Western Mahayana), and China, Japan, Korea and Hawaii (Eastern Mahayana), cp. *Hinayana*. The Mahayana gradually developed from the primitive teaching, and no sharp line of demarcation has ever existed.

MANAS: Mind; the rational faculty in man. That aspect of consciousness (*viññana*) concerned with the relation of subject and object. Manas is essentially dual, its lower aspect being concerned with and directed towards the worlds of sense; and the higher, attracted to and illumined by *bodhi*, the faculty of intuition. This latter, differentiated by the term *bodhicitta*, is the storehouse of the experiences of the past and is the individuality, the viññana which creates the bodies and environment of the next life on earth.

MYSTICISM: the recognition of the essential unity of life, and of conscious attainment of complete individual harmony with that unity.

Mystical philosophy is based on the concept of a transcendental monistic noumenon expressing itself through the diversity of the phenomenal. Mystical religion is the striving for complete conscious harmony with that ultimate unity: its goal is, therefore, *experience of Reality*.

This doctrine is innate in Hinayana Buddhism; Anatta and Nirvana being its philosophical and religious bases. In the Mahayana School these doctrines are elaborated into a variety of forms, all endeavouring to express these fundamental truths in aspects which may appeal to every stage of mental growth and spiritual development, the one precept of all being "Look within thee, thou art Buddha!"

NETI, NETI: "Not this, not this."

NIRVANA (Sk.) NIBBANA (P.): The supreme Goal of Buddhist endeavour; release from the limitations of existence. The word is derived from a root which signifies "extinguished through lack of fuel", and since re-birth is the result of egoistic desire (*tanha*), freedom from rebirth is attained by the extinguishing of all such desire. Nirvana is, therefore, a state attainable in this life by right aspiration, purity of life, and the elimination of egoism. One who has attained to this state is called a saint or arhat (q.v.), and at the death of his physical body attains complete or final nirvana (*parinibbana* or *anupadisesa nirvana*) in which all attributes relating to phenomenal existence cease, and which is, therefore, called *sunyata* or void. This is cessation of existence, as we know existence; the attainment of Being (as distinct from becoming); union with Ultimate Reality. This is the goal of all mystic endeavour, and mystics of every creed speak of it as "a state which passeth all understanding". In the Buddhist scriptures (*Udana* ch. 8, p. 112 of Strong's trsl.) the Buddha speaks of it as "an unborn, unoriginated, uncreated, unformed", contrasting it with the born, originated, created and formed phenomenal world.

The Hinayana School tends to view Nirvana as escape from life by overcoming its attractions: the Mahayana views it as the fruition of life—the unfolding of the infinite possibilities of the innate Buddha-nature—, and exalts the saint who remains in touch with life, rather than the saint who relinquishes all connection with it.

PÂLI: One of the "sacred" languages of Buddhism. The language in which the Pitakas or Pâli Canon of the Hinayana School were first committed to writing.

PARAMITAS: Perfections. The Six (or ten) stages of spiritual perfection followed by the Bodhisattva in his progress to Buddhahood. They include the practice and highest possible development of charity, morality, patient resignation, zeal, meditation and contemplation, wisdom. The following four are sometimes added: skilful means of teaching, power over obstacles, spiritual aspiration, and knowledge, these last four being, however, regarded as amplifications of *Prajña,* wisdom.

PITAKAS: Pitaka=basket. The Buddhist Pâli Canon is called the Pitakas, or the Tipitaka (three baskets). These are called Sutta P., Abhidhamma P., and Vinaya P. Applied in the sense of "handing on", as baskets are used to hand on earth in excavation work.

REBIRTH: The intermittent functioning of the entity in any one of the various phenomenal worlds, under karmic law. The continuous process of "becoming".

RUPA: Form. ARUPA, formless. Form implies limitation, and form as cognized by the lower mind persists into the lower heaven worlds. The higher heaven worlds are called formless because the mind is free from the limitations of the senses. Desire for life in the worlds of form (*ruparaga*) is the sixth Fetter to be cast off, and *aruparaga* the seventh.

SAKKAYADITTHI: The belief that in one or all of the five *Skandhas* (q.v.) there is an individuality or self, an *atta*. The first of the Ten Fetters.

SAMADHI: Contemplation on Reality. The state of spiritual ecstasy consequent on complete elimination of all sense of separateness, resulting from continued meditation on Reality. It is superior to meditation in that the three factors of meditation (the mind of the individual, the object of meditation, and the relationship between them) are transcended. *Samma samadhi*, perfect contemplation, is the last stage of the Noble Eightfold Path, and the prelude to Nirvana.

SAMSARA: Lit. 'faring on', continued 'coming-to be.' Samsara, as *Existence*, is contrasted with Nirvana, *Being*, the one being subject to all the limitations of "becoming", the other being the state of pure "Being" (or Be-ness). Nirvana is symbolically referred to as "the further shore of the ocean of samsara"; the *dhamma* as the raft which carries us across.

SANGHA: An Assembly. The monastic order founded by the Buddha, the members of which are called bhikkhus (m) or bhikkhunis (f). It is the oldest monastic order in the world. No oaths are taken, and the bhikkhu is free to leave the Order at any time if he desires to do so. The bhikkhu possesses only his robes, alms-bowl, razor, needle and water-strainer. He eats only one meal a day, no food being taken after mid-day.

In the Mahayana School, the Sangha tends to become recognized as a spiritual unity rather than a physical one. The ideal Sangha is the community of followers of the

Dhamma in the world, rather than an exclusive few who retire from the world. The monastic system was strong in Tibet, but is dying out in China and Japan. Monasteries exist in most M. sects, but they are training colleges for *bhikkhus* rather than retreats from the world. Bhikkhus of M. sects keep few Vinaya Rules, and often marry. They are teachers rather than monks.

SELF: Atman (atta): the Supreme SELF; Universal Consciousness; Ultimate Reality; the Buddha-nature, or Essence of Mind in man. The degradation of this latter into the idea of an entity (soul, ego) dwelling in the heart of each man, the thinker of his thoughts, the doer of his deeds and after death dwelling in bliss or misery according to deeds done in the body is utterly rejected by Buddhism. To avoid misconception Buddhists usually shun the term 'soul'; where they do use it, it connotes the character created by experience in the phenomenal worlds, and even becoming more and more enlightened by following the Path, or more degraded by departing from it.

SIDDHIS (P., Iddhis): Supernormal powers developed in following the path to arhatship: these include clairvoyance, clairaudience, telepathy, recalling one's former lives, etc. It is forbidden to use these psychic powers (the lower iddhis) for one's personal benefit. The higher iddhis are the spiritual Modes of Mystic Insight attained by the practice of dhyana.

SIGNS OF BEING: *Anicca* (impermanence), *Dukkha* (dissatisfaction, suffering) and *Anatta* (doctrine of non-ego).

SILA: Moral precepts, code of morality, Buddhist ethics. Pancha-sila, the Five Precepts; dasa-sila, the ten Precepts. One of the moral 'Trinity' of Sila, right deeds, Dana, benevolence, Bhavana, purification and discipline of the mind, from which Pañña, wisdom, follows.

SKANDHAS (*Khandhâ* (P.) *Skandhâ* (Sk.)): The five causally conditioned elements of existence forming a being or entity. In the personal sense, the skandhas are the elements which condition the appearance of life in any form; which together make up the personality in the sphere of Samsara. The Five Skandhas are inherent in every form of life, either in an active or a potential state, *e.g.*, there is consciousness in the mineral, but it is dormant. In man, all five elements are active. These are enumerated as: 1, *Rupa*; 2, *Vedanâ*; 3, *Saññâ*; 4, *Sankhârâ*; 5, *Viññâna*.

These are all material, in the sense of being subject to the characteristics of existence, *anicca, dukkha, anatta.* They form the temporal or phenomenal nature of man, and it is the idea or belief that separately or collectively they form a self or ego that is the heresy of *sakayaditthi*, the first of the Ten Fetters which bind men to the Wheel of Life.

SUTTA (P.), SUTRA (Sk.): a thread or string (on which jewels are strung), thus applied to that part of the Pâli Canon containing the narratives about dialogues by the Buddha. The *Sutta Pitaka* consists of the five 'Nikayas', i.e., Digha, Majjhima, Samyutta, Anguttara, Khuddaka. There are also a number of Mahayana scriptures called *sutras*.

THERAVADA (P.): The 'doctrine of the Elders'. The only one to survive of the eighteen sects of the Hinayana (q.v.), the earliest Buddhist school. Its complete Canon exists in Pâli, now translated into English. The school is found in Ceylon, Burma, Thailand and Cambodia. Therefore sometimes called the Southern School of Buddhism.

WHEEL OF LIFE (*Bhavachakra*): The Wheel has been used by many religions as the symbol of the ever-rolling activity of life. Buddhism adopted the same symbol to typify the ceaseless process of becoming and its limitation (finiteness). It conceives of man as bound to this Wheel so long as he thinks of him(self) as bound, but when he attains a realization that the 'self' he thinks of is an illusory 'self', he is freed from the Wheel and attains liberation into that state of infinity called Nirvana.

YOGA: A word meaning "yoke", in the sense of "that which unites", therefore "union" and the system of discipline which brings a man to union with Reality.

NOTE: Many other terms are explained in the text. For fuller Glossary see *A Popular Dictionary of Buddhism*, Christmas Humphreys, Arco Publications 1962.

Index

(See also Contents and Glossary)